W9-ALX-389

FORRESTER'S

Wine in Words

For Roger, always

Wine in Words

NOTES FOR
BETTER
DRINKING

Lettie Teague

ILLUSTRATIONS BY WACSO

Rizzoli
ex libris

First published in the United States of America in 2015
by Rizzoli Ex Libris, an imprint of
Rizzoli International Publications, Inc.
300 Park Avenue South
New York, NY 10010
www.rizzoliusa.com

© 2015 Lettie Teague

Illustrations ©WACSO
Design by Vertigo Design NYC

All rights reserved. No part of this publication may be reproduced, stored in a retrieval system,
or transmitted in any form or by any means, electronic, mechanical, photocopying,
recording, or otherwise, without prior consent of the publishers.

2015 2016 2017 2018 / 10 9 8 7 6 5 4 3 2 1

Distributed in the U.S. trade by Random House, New York

PRINTED IN CHINA

ISBN-13: 978-0-8478-4543-9

Library of Congress Control Number: 2014956302

Contents

Introduction

A BOOK OF ESSAYS SHOULD BE READ SLOWLY over a period of time—a week perhaps or even a month. Like a good wine (an inevitable analogy), a book of essays should be savored, not gulped. To extend the wine analogy further (just once, I promise), it's a bit like an open bottle of tawny Port. Unlike a regular bottle of wine or even vintage Port, a tawny Port can last a long time—as long as a month. Tawny Port doesn't deteriorate in the way that a bottle of regular will because it's made in a purposely pre-oxidative style. (There are some practical tips like that in this book too.)

There's also an essay that includes Port. It's one of my favorite dessert wines—along with its stylistic opposite, Moscato. There are essays about some of my least favorite wines too (see under: South African Pinotage) and wines that other people hate so much that they even formed a club (ABC or Anything But Chardonnay).

There are essays about practical stuff like buying, storing, and collecting wine as well and matching wine and food—especially cheese. Were ever two things more often combined, or at least talked about, as cheese and wine?

There are also essays about wines at weddings and the best wines to give as presents (hint: when in doubt, supersize). Both topics come up over and over again in everyday life, and yet I can count on one hand the number of weddings I've attended where good wine was served. Why do people spend so much on flowers and so little on wine? The one exception seems to be Champagne—most brides and grooms seem willing to spend a bit on their wedding Champagne. Maybe that's why it's the only wine they can actually remember.

There are profiles of a few of my favorite wine regions such as Sicily and Napa and Sonoma and Chablis. There could probably be a lot more of these since I don't think I've visited a wine region that I haven't liked and wanted to visit again and again. Wine regions are almost by definition desirable places. I'm ever mindful of the fact that the places that others visit on vacation are invariably the places I visit for work.

There are essays about winery dogs and plenty of essays about people. In a way, of course, every essay in this book is about a person in one way or another—winemakers, winery owners, wine collectors, retailers, wholesalers, and sommeliers. And wine lovers who like to read about wine. As the wine columnist for *The Wall Street Journal* and prior to that, the wine columnist for *Food & Wine* magazine, I am especially indebted to the wine lovers who are also wine readers. This book is for you.

A vine that doesn't have
to work hard will create
an innocuous wine—
much in the same way
that a life of leisure may
produce a ne'er-do-well.

Fun to Know

The Well-Dressed Wine

I DON'T RECALL THE EXACT MOMENT when wine transitioned from a beverage to be consumed to a glass of something that needed to be adorned, but it happened some years ago when I wasn't paying much attention. And now every other glass of wine that I'm served at a party seems to have some sort of gimcrack or geegaw on the stem or the base of the glass. I'm talking about wine accessories, of course.

A particular favorite of a friend are the bits of plastic "jewelry" that encircle the glass stem. "Now you can tell which glass is yours," my friend—and many other hostesses—have said to me as she handed me a glass to which she'd attached something that looked like a plastic doll shoe.

Never mind that wine drinkers have managed to keep track of their glasses for many hundreds of years without resorting to plastic doll shoes as identity clues. Or that maybe they didn't want to think about shoes while drinking a glass of Pétrus.

And decorated glassware is just the beginning of this seemingly endless wine accessories binge. There are battery-powered corkscrews that light up at night (just in case the electricity goes out or the conversation lulls?) and there are pens that you can use to draw pictures right on the glass. There are even "outfits" for the bottles themselves—the kind that children once liked to put on the family dog.

The wine accessories business actually seems to have a lot in common with the pet industry. The same sort of people who buy clothes for their pugs are probably buying rhinestones to "enhance" their Merlot.

And yet all this adornment won't alter the fact of a wine (or a dog, for that matter) that's no good. A bag or a ring or a bit of writing on the glass is at best a distraction. And with a good wine in hand, the last thing that a drinker wants is to be distracted from the wine in the glass. That's far worse than finding out halfway through dinner that the glass you've been drinking from isn't actually your own.

Around the Watering Hole

PEOPLE TALK ABOUT WINE IN ALL KINDS OF WAYS. There's conversation that takes place over a meal, which may be about the merits or the pitfalls of a particular pairing. There's the chat in a wine shop or restaurant with a merchant or sommelier when a recommendation is needed or some insight into a particular producer or vintage is sought. There are conversations that take place in winery tasting rooms but they're often one-sided. (Would-be tasters hold out glasses and the staff describes what they should expect to find inside: "Hints of cherry, dark fruit, and vanilla.")

But some of the most interesting conversations about wine are ones that I've "overheard" online over the years, via Twitter and in chat rooms and on bulletin boards. There are so many opinions and stories about wine that you are unlikely to develop or experience on your own. And while I've never initiated a topic, I've eavesdropped on thousands of stimulating chats. (I do what in Internet parlance is called "lurking"; that's when someone just reads what others are saying without ever posting any comments.)

There are all kinds of interesting (and some not-so-interesting) topics under discussion. They are often leavened by a bit of wine world gossip—such as whether or not a particular wine merchant buys certain bottles from the gray market (where wine is unofficially bought and sold) or if a Pinot Noir grower actually buys some of his grapes.

I've found winemakers that I'd never heard of before and descriptions of wine regions that I've always wanted to visit. I've read opinions about vintages—whether the 1989 or 1990 Bordeaux is better—and a lot about wines that have been tasted. I've read passionate paeans to Champagne and denunciations of Syrah or Napa Cabernet or white wines from the Rhône (and on and on). I've also read sad exchanges of experiences about wines that were corked.

There are occasional acerbic exchanges about certain professionals and critics. (The famed Robert M. Parker, Jr., comes in for a lashing over and over again, although he has his defenders, not to mention the bulletin board on the website that bears his name.) There are even regular plans for members to get together in person—to carry on the very same sorts of conversations live, over real bottles.

It's a bit like stopping by the community pool (or perhaps the local bar would be a better analogy) to hear what a lot of like-minded and some not-so-like-minded people are thinking. I plan to jump into the pool, pull up a bar stool, one day soon.

The Back Story

ONCE UPON A TIME, NOT SO LONG AGO, the back label was where you would find just about everything you needed to know about a bottle of wine. There was the improbably wide pairing advice ("Drink with pasta, chicken, beef, and fish.") There was the inevitable personal anecdote ("I found this vineyard after years of searching all over the world" or "I inherited it from a great-aunt three times removed").

There was usually some information about the winemaking process and the type of barrels that played a starring role. Barrels are expensive, after all, especially new French ones, so they're usually cited in large, impressive type. (Perhaps it's the producer's way of noting the price.) There is usually a bit of additional narrative here too: "This wine spent six months/a year/a decade in new French oak."

And there was usually the application of a few adverbs. The wine was inevitably made "carefully" or "lovingly" or even "judiciously" by the winemaker in question. And in some cases, the back labels even invoked the name of the winery dog—or better yet depicted said canine as well. And what hard-hearted drinker wouldn't want to buy a wine from a winemaker in possession of a cute winery dog?

Sometimes there was a map, especially if the wine came from some place other than California. (Actually some California wine bottles came adorned with maps although they were usually from well-known places like Sonoma or Napa. I suspect these maps are more geographical bragging rights than location guides.)

Few of these things appear very often on back labels of bottles these days. Sadly it seems that most of today's back labels are less romantic or folksy or even food-centric. Instead they feature the names of the men who imported or distributed or even selected them—some of whom are even bold enough to put their names on the front: "A Wine Chosen by Fill-in-the-Blank." (I won't shame the importers by naming names, but you know who you are.)

It's the accomplishments and histories and even philosophies of these men that appear on back labels today. (Yes, in fact, they all seem to be men: the female importers must be much more modest.) There's no pairing advice or talk about barrels or a map and they almost never show a picture of the winery dog. And while I do think that some of these importers have very good taste in selecting and importing certain wines, as a dog lover and a map reader I still think their absence from the back label is a bit of a loss.

Tasting Blind

OF ALL THE ARCANE ASPECTS OF WINE, none may be more mysterious and maybe more useless than the act of blind tasting. While wine professionals consider blind tasting a wine an ideal way to determine a wine's quality free of the kind of prejudice a label might produce, it's also a fun way to humiliate wine-drinking friends.

Actually a blind tasting can be an effective tool of humiliation for wine professionals, too, and I've been on both the giving and receiving end. I've tricked famous sommeliers by offering wines to taste blind and been tricked by them in turn. The good news for would-be tricksters is that many wines taste like many others; for example, a Washington State Merlot can taste very much like a Napa Valley Cabernet. Ditto a New Zealand Sauvignon Blanc and a Sancerre or even a Grüner Veltliner and Pinot Grigio. (Yes, I've tricked friends with all of those wines.)

I could go and on about these trickster wines but instead, and perhaps more usefully, I will describe—briefly—what constitutes a blind tasting and what a blind tasting is (theoretically) meant to effect.

The "blind" part means that the name on the label and even the bottles themselves are hidden from view—most often shrouded in cloth or brown paper bags. The bottle is hidden too, because even its shape can provide a valuable clue. For example, a Burgundy bottle is rounded and slope-shouldered and generally contains wines made from Burgundy grapes (Pinot Noir and Chardonnay). A Bordeaux bottle is more upright and rectangular and usually contains Cabernet and Merlot blends or grapes. A narrow Riesling bottle generally holds aromatic wines like Gewürztraminer and Riesling. (Of course, some winemakers like to switch things up—put Bordeaux-style wines in Burgundy bottles—so there is always the possibility that there is a false clue in the bottles.)

Most blind tastings are conducted so that attendees have some idea about the general category of wines that they're tasting. For example, the blind tasting might include Napa Valley Cabernets or Russian River Chardonnays from Sonoma. This is arguably a more useful sort of tasting than one that is totally blind, since it gives tasters a way to compare wines of the same type against one another.

It's definitely of greater utility than a so-called double-blind tasting, where the tasters don't know anything at all—not the grape nor the region nor the country. I've only attended two of these, but they were pretty ridiculous exercises: men making all sorts of random-sounding observations about the wines—it was more like free-association than an actual tasting of wine. For some reason men seem to be more frequently found in blind tastings. Whether that means they're braver or more foolhardy, I don't know. But they seem to be more willing to try to identify a wine whose label is concealed.

And that's a big part of blind tasting. In some ways it's more about the words, the artfulness of the description, than about actually identifying the wine. There is a particular scene in the documentary movie *Somm* that captures this fact perfectly. Four sommeliers (men) who are competing for the title Master Sommelier are asked to describe a wine blind and they recite a line of seemingly unrelated words in an almost trancelike state: "clean youthful high intensity notes of lanolin mandarin grapefruit pith lemon seeds lime skin," they intone.

But perhaps that's what blind tasting should actually produce: a broadening of one's vocabulary of wine descriptions. That would be a truly useful skill, and in fact, the better you are able to describe a particular wine, the better you can communicate with a wine retailer or a sommelier and get a wine that you'll like.

In fact, I'd really like to see someone order a wine the way these sommeliers talk—not in terms of grapes or place names but by pure descriptors alone: "I'd like a wine with notes of lanolin mandarin grapefruit pith lemon seeds and lime skin—for under fifty bucks."

Bottle Braggarts

WHY DO SO MANY COLLECTORS have such an overwhelming desire to show off their wines? Why do they want other people to know what they have? Why do they check out one another's collections on websites and feel a need to make a status exchange? Naturally this includes a good bit of one upsmanship of numbers and names. (Sample collector quote: "I have two cases of 1982 Mouton Rothschild." Counter-quote: "I have every vintage of La Mouline since 1978.")

I recently met a wine collector at an open house in my town. After the real estate agent introduced us, the collector barely registered my name, but when he found out that I was a wine writer, he immediately suggested that I stop over to have a look at his cellar. Not to have a conversation or, better, a taste of what he owned—just a viewing of the bottles he'd managed to amass over the past couple decades.

This was just the beginning of this particular one-sided conversation. He followed up his invitation with the story of his collection and how he came to acquire it. "I started out collecting Napa Cabernet, progressed to Bordeaux, and eventually began buying Burgundy," the man said, describing a standard trajectory of so many wine collectors that it's practically a script. He cited a number of specific names, rare or expensive—and most often both.

My role in this exchange was simply as a witness who was given an opportunity to occasionally nod and remark at the collector's particular perspicacity and daring—and seemingly unlimited funds. These kinds of collectors always appreciate a comment or two thrown their way like a verbal bone, especially if it includes one or more of following words: *amazing*, *spectacular*, or *that must be worth a lot.*

Actually I don't need to say that last phrase at all because such collectors will more often than not tell me exactly how much they paid for a bottle—and how much (more) said bottle is worth today. If wine is something to be shared, then a trophy cellar is something to be talked about.

If these tours actually take place, they sometimes include something to drink; some generous collectors like to tell their guests to choose whatever wine they'd like. A larger number of collectors are likely to direct you to particular parts of the cellar where the "lesser" wines reside and suggest you choose from their ranks. Some collectors offer nothing but a show.

Whether generous or stingy or somewhere in between, these collectors don't seem to have a correlative among collectors of other things. Take, for example, collectors of fine shoes and handbags. While I know women who have many fine specimens of both, I've never once heard them say to me (or, for that matter, a stranger), "You really ought to have a look at my closet. I've got some really great Gucci and Louis Vuitton," and I've yet to hear someone recount how they started with Hush Puppies and worked their way up to Manolo Blahnik.

Maybe it's because shoes and handbags can be worn and therefore can be noticed all by themselves, while you can't exactly sling a case of Mouton over your shoulder and go for a walk. Or maybe, in the best instances, it's that wine collectors are essentially gregarious and (some) are quite generous and want to share the wealth.

The Cheese Rules

OF ALL THE FOOD AND WINE COMBINATIONS IN THE WORLD, I can't think of one that is more frequently, more lovingly, or more exhaustively described than the marriage of wine and cheese. Other pairings may evoke interest and even attention, but only cheese and wine can inspire real scholarship.

What is it about the two together that warrants such devoted scrutiny? Is cheese truly that much more interesting than any other food in the world or is it because there are so many hundreds, even thousands of cheeses made in so many places around the world? In other words, is the appeal actually mathematical too—how many combinations can be made of all the thousands of cheeses with all the hundreds of thousands of wines?

I like cheese and I like wine and sometimes I even enjoy putting them together—but I don't think overmuch about it (perhaps because I'm not very good at math?). I don't agonize about whether or not Sauvignon Blanc should be paired with a cheese that's hard or soft or, for that matter, cheese that's sheep or goat.

One frequently cited solution for people like me, who are looking for the easy way out or at least some sort of respectable shortcut, is to consider where the cheese and the wine came from and put them together that way. For example, Sancerre and goat cheese both come from the same place in the world (the Loire Valley of France), and their combo works pretty well. There are lots of others examples—like Parmigiano Reggiano, a salty cow's milk cheese produced in the Emilia-Romagna region that actually goes very nicely with the region's sparkling reds (Lambrusco).

But what of cheeses with no wine counterpart? What wine do you pair with, say, a cheddar cheese from Vermont? I figured a cheese professional might have greater insight, so I put the question to Anne Saxelby, a young cheesemonger in New York with a store full of cheeses and a passionate following. Were there pairing rules Ms. Saxelby could pass along?

Ms. Saxelby it turned out, was a great believer in cheese and wine geography. "If two products come from the same place they probably go together," she wrote in an email, although she acknowledged this was tricky too (see under: Vermont). But in that case she said that she followed a more anarchic "rule": "Just have fun."

This was advice that even the math adverse like me could follow. And if the pairing didn't work—that is, it wasn't fun—I'd add one piece of advice: Make sure you give up the cheese—not the wine—first.

Catch the Bubble Wave

THERE ARE MORE PEOPLE DRINKING SPARKLING WINES from more places in the world than ever before, and more people making these wines as well. There might be more sparkling wine produced and consumed than ever before in the history of wine: I don't have statistics to prove it, but sales of sparkling wines from all over the world are definitely up—in a very big way.

And the phenomenon is truly global in scope. The Italians are having huge success with Prosecco and Moscato, and even Lambrusco, the red sparkling wine from Emilia-Romagna, is having a renaissance. There's also serious sparkling wine from the Franciacorta region of Lombardy, whose producers like to compare their equally expensive wines to those of Champagne.

And in Spain, there is a veritable tsunami of Cava being produced in the Penedès region near Barcelona. The list of sparkling-specific wines from various countries goes on and on: Austria, Germany, Argentina, New Zealand, and Brazil (whose winemakers are actually quite serious about sparkling wine; their sparklers are their flagship exports).

There's the United States, of course, where sparkling wines are made in numerous states from just about every noble—or otherwise—grape. There's France, too, where every region that isn't Champagne makes a sparkling version of its native wines—including, rather remarkably, Bordeaux.

What does this (all) mean? That wine drinkers everywhere are looking for more reasons to celebrate? Or that they have finally figured out that a sparkling wine actually goes well with food. (This is particularly true of sparkling Rosé, which has the double advantage of a bit of body and fruitiness, too.)

American wine drinkers have definitely acquired a taste for the bubbly; in fact, not long ago (in 2012), sparkling wine sales were their highest since 1987—aka the year of the second-worst American stock market crash. (Champagne also happened to be selling well just before the first crash—and the Great Depression; it was the drink of choice for the famous and the glamorous in Hollywood.)

Might sparkling wine sales have some greater significance—could they even be a bellwether of sorts for history? Only time will tell if this is true. In the meantime there's a lot of really good sparkling wine around—and no better time to drink it than now.

Drink or Keep

I BUY WINE, I DRINK WINE, but I don't collect wine. I'm more of an accumulator than I am a collector. And yet every so often when I look at the hundreds of bottles that I somehow managed to acquire, I wonder if I might have inadvertently built some sort of a collection?

There is definitely a difference between collecting and accumulating, starting with a question of intent. A collector has a particular reason in mind when he (or she) is buying. It's not just about having something appealing to drink. This consideration generally includes a fiscal component, since most collectible wine appreciates in value over time. Some collectors will buy wines with this fact foremost in mind. They may not intend to drink them at all—they just want to hold on to them until the value of the bottles increases ten- or twenty-fold and sell them when the market is good.

There were a number of "wine funds" created in recent years (mostly in London) with this sort of collector in mind. Wine funds had managers like any other fund except that they bought bottles of "blue chip" Bordeaux instead of company shares. It was a sexy idea, but alas most failed to make any money—the basic principal of investment—so they didn't last very long. A bottle of Château Haut-Brion, however amazing, just doesn't do ROR (rate of return) the way Apple and Amazon do.

Collecting wine also helps to ensure that a wine drinker will have an aged wine on hand that's ready to drink—though there's no guarantee that said drinker will guess right and open a bottle at the exact right time. I will bet that far too many collectors have waited too long to open a bottle rather than too short a time. (And so have lots of noncollectors,

like my friends who keep their wines under their stairs.) And then there is the question of whether or not the wine will get better at all, since only a tiny fraction of the world's wines actually improve with age.

A wine collection is also determined by the type of storage facility. Wine cannot be considered "collected" unless it's stored in a proper place. That generally means a temperature-controlled warehouse, cellar, or cave. I have two temperature-controlled units in my basement, but I also have wines that just sit on shelves. These shelves are in that same cool, dark basement room, but they aren't in a collector-worthy space. These are wines that only an accumulator could love. (No auction house will buy wines from a private collection that haven't been properly stored.)

A collector also has a system to keep track of bottles, whether it's on a computer or a handwritten list. A collector's list is accurate and up to date. An accumulater just has a bunch of bottles that he or she pulls out and examines occasionally, not sure if it will turn out to be Pinot Noir or Cabernet. An accumulator's cellar is the vinous equivalent of a messy desk whose occupant says that he (or she) "knows where everything is."

Wine accumulators rarely pay attention to the critics' scores. Collectors need to know at all times what the wine critics think, with an eye toward resale value. Accumulators can have wild enthusiasms and buy wines that, on paper at least, may not seem to make sense. They can fall in love with Italian Sylvaners or California Chenin Blancs or even fruit wines from New Jersey—wines they love without thought of their status in the world. But there's one thing that both wine accumulators and wine collectors know how to do: drink.

Champagne Wishes

WHAT IS THE TRUE MEASURE OF FAME? Starring in your own television show? Having your face on the front of a box of breakfast cereal? I think it's when your name becomes an adjective. Take, for example, Sigmund Freud. Who hasn't heard of—or for that matter, been guilty of—a Freudian slip?

There is only one wine so famous that it became an adjective employed all over the world. Who doesn't know what it means to lead a Champagne lifestyle or possess what some would describe as "Champagne taste"? There are even Champagne-colored dresses (often favored for bridesmaids and brides).

There isn't any other wine that resonates quite as meaningfully as this great sparkling wine from France. But why? What sets Champagne apart and makes it sought after by serious collectors and casual drinkers alike?

There is both a short and a long answer to those questions. The short answer is that there is nothing else quite like it. There are lots of different types of sparkling wines, some even made by the same method, but nothing that quite measures up. The long answer, as you might expect, expands on that fact. Champagne makers will gladly provide a long list of the reasons why their sparkler is superior. I'll offer a few.

One of the most important reasons has to do with the place where it's made. Located in a far northerly region of France less than two hours from Paris, Champagne has a distinct, chalky white soil and a punishing environment that presents a particular hardship for grapes that often have trouble ripening. (The grapes are almost invariably some combination of these three—Chardonnay, Pinot Noir, and Pinot Meunier—although technically others are permitted as well.)

If this were a non-sparkling wine region like Burgundy (its neighbor), then less-than-ripe grapes might be a problem. But Champagne actually requires wines with lots of acidity; if the area were warmer, the acidity levels of the grapes would not be as high.

The production of Champagne also requires a great deal of skill. It's not just a matter of growing the grapes then fermenting and bottling the wine. It's a multistep process that requires all the work of regular winemaking plus extra complications like blending the wines, introducing the second fermentation, trapping the gas in the bottle (which makes the wine sparkle), then aging it for a specified amount of time—sometimes years and sometimes even decades. (This isn't something that a maker of Prosecco would want or could afford to do.)

And yet for all the hard work that goes into making Champagne, more is made of what the wine looks like than how it tastes. This is to say, what matters mightily is the packaging and the name. Drinkers reference the Champagne with the orange label (Veuve Clicquot) or the Champagne of Dom Pérignon (Moët & Chandon) or maybe the Champagne in the tiny bottle called POP (that's Pommery). More than any other wine in the world, Champagne encourages the people who love it to think of it in terms of a brand.

Make a Fake

PLINY THE ELDER was famously a philosopher and statesman in ancient Rome, but he was also a bit of a detective when it came to wine fraud. It was Pliny the Elder who pointed out to his peers around A.D. 70 that the Falernian wine they were drinking wasn't all it was cracked up be. The wine was fake, according to Pliny—even if it isn't clear (from what I've read) that Pliny was actually outraged by the fakery as much as by the credulousness of the drinkers. Pliny's message seems to be that nobility should not have to wonder if their wine is real.

In a few thousand years very little has changed. Fake wine is still on the minds of rich men (and a few women), although instead of having philosophers champion their cause, they hire fancy lawyers to file expensive lawsuits. Two of the most prominent cases of wine fraud in the past few years have involved one billionaire (Bill Koch) and one fake millionaire (Rudy Kurniawan), who went from buying expensive wines from others to making his own.

In Mr. Koch's case, he found that a large number of expensive wines in his collection, including a bottle of 1864 Château Latour, were in fact fraudulent. He filed lawsuits against the auction house where he purchased them as well as the individual collector and, after seven years, finally won a $12 million settlement against the collector, which was eventually reduced to less than $1 million.

For Mr. Kurniawan, it was a matter of figuring out how to belong to a rich men's club. Although he rose to prominence as a collector of great wines that were presumably real, he realized he could make even more friends—and a lot more money—if he came up with a way to make his own. So he crafted and sold "rare" bottles of counterfeit Burgundy and Bordeaux.

These are just two-high profile cases; there is fraudulent wine made everywhere, every day, and it's not all rare and expensive wine. There have been fake wine scandals involving Beaujolais, and fake Pinot Noir created by Gallo (a brand called Red Bicyclette that turned out to be Merlot and Syrah), and there was of course the famous so-called anti-freeze incident in Austria in the 1980s, where some unscrupulous and almost homicidal types doctored up some Austrian wine with diethylene glycol (the compound in antifreeze) to make it taste sweeter. That scandal pretty much killed the Austrian wine business for a while; fortunately no Austrian wine drinkers actually died. By the way, this was an exception: fake wine is rarely fatal—it's more often just not very good.

And there have been plenty of other scandals in other parts of the world: fake Brunellos, fake Champagnes, and of course fake wine investment schemes. As long as there is real wine there will be fake wine. At least one thing, however, has changed—and for the fraudsters, at least, it's for the better. Whereas wine fraud was once considered so heinous an act that fraudsters were beaten and sometimes even hanged, now they may have to simply pay a fine or while away a few years in prison. And perhaps when they get out, they can get a job as an appraiser for a wine auction house or enroll in winemaking school. Who knows the worth—or the profile—of a great wine better than someone who has "made" one himself?

On the House

HOW'S THE HOUSE WINE? It's a question that no one seems to ask much anymore. Not only in restaurants but everywhere else. House wine isn't something that people I know seem to keep in their house. There is only one person who has ever offered me a glass of what she called her "house wine"—and I can remember only one time that I ordered a house wine off a wine list.

Some people might consider this a positive change. A house wine, after all, was what restaurant diners relied on in the bad old days when wine was something most people regarded as scary and foreign. They just wanted something that was white or red—preferably from a prestigious-sounding country like France.

A house wine was also a good way for a restaurant to make (a lot of) money, since it was an anonymous brand that they could mark up a thousand times if they felt like it. If no one knew the name, no one would know how much it should cost. A house wine was a big revenue boost.

Now most restaurants offer wines by the glass (and signature cocktails) because people are much better educated about wine and want lots of choices. These wines are pretty well marked up, so restaurants still make pretty good revenue.

But I miss the idea of what a house wine can be at its very best: something inherently personal, a wine that is the true signature of a person or a place. The one person I know who has a house wine is my sister, Arian. Her house wine is Kim Crawford Sauvignon Blanc, a wine from New Zealand. She actually has two in her house, since her husband Joe's signature wine is Blue Nun—that fad wine of the '70s. Joe has cases and cases of Blue Nun in his pantry, seemingly afraid that one day they might stop making it.

I know that every time that I visit their house those are the two wines that they will serve—almost exclusively. While I can't say much about the Blue Nun (I've tried it a few times and found it a bit sickly sweet), the Kim Crawford is reliable and solid, crisp and refreshing if not particularly exciting. It's not too expensive or too cheap—just under fifteen dollars a bottle.

These wines taste the same year in, year out, and my sister appreciates that kind of reliability. After all, there is so much that *isn't* reliable in life, she likes to have something dependable even if it's just a wine in a glass. She will try other wines when I bring them along, and she will usually enjoy them—but she's always happy to retreat to her house brand.

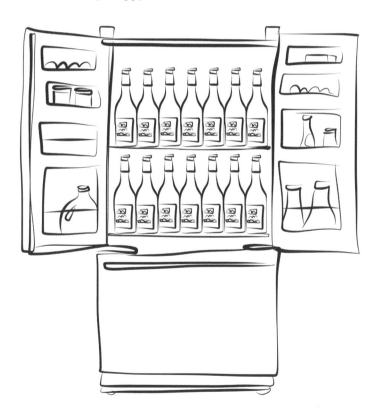

The End of the Cults

ONCE UPON A TIME, NOT SO LONG AGO, the surest mark of success for a California winemaker was to be lauded as a "cult wine" creator. Although originally coined to describe a very specific sort of Cabernet produced in the Napa Valley, *cult* soon became the word of choice to describe every sought-after wine in the world.

A cult Napa Cabernet earned its status by fulfilling several key criteria. The first was that it had to be produced in very small amounts—preferably a thousand cases or fewer. The fruit had to be ultra-ripe and the wine had to be super-concentrated in character. (In fact those words were practically required to appear in the winemaker's notes.) And the winemaker him- or herself had to be a boldfaced name who consulted to wineries all over Napa if not the world and charged a very large—at least six-figure—fee.

The winery owner had to be a magnate of some sort or another, preferably from a non-wine world like tech or banking, the sort that could be described at length by the cult publicist. And this magnate could not be shy about lending the cult wine his name and attaching a mid-three-figure price tag. The final criteria was a high score. A cult wine had to be sanctioned by the powerful wine critics, who would hopefully bestow at least 96 points on the wine—it could never be less. (Who builds a cult around something less than nearly perfect, after all?)

The cult business turned out to be such a great model that other wine producers decided to follow suit with their "cult" Pinots and "cult" Chardonnays and even "cult" Rieslings. Cult wines were issued from all kinds of grapes from other parts of the world. A cult Muscadet suddenly seemed like it wasn't completely unlikely or absurd.

And yet no one stopped to ask why wine drinkers (and winemakers and wine promoters)—why anyone would want to drink or make or promote something as being worthy of a cult?

After all, the word *cult* is defined as a "system of veneration, directed toward a particular figure or object," and it has a rather unhealthy ring in the "regular" world. I wonder if even the most rabid oenophile actually believes that a wine is truly deserving of worship, let alone veneration. As much as I love a good bottle of Cabernet or Chardonnay or even Muscadet, I don't want to deify it.

Happily, the era of cults—wines, that is—seems to have faded somewhat. Perhaps that's inevitable when a word becomes so overused that there is an actual business called Cult Wine that sells the wines they have identified as cult-worthy—including some of the usual Napa cult Cabs (Scarecrow and Screaming Eagle, for example) but also wines like Dom Pérignon, which I've seen sold in grocery stores. Or maybe the end of the cult is truly near when one winemaker actually advertised his services as a "cult winemaker" . . . in a classified ad.

Natural Enough

ONE OF THE MOST BENIGN-SEEMING ADJECTIVES is at the heart of one of the biggest controversies in the wine world today. When the adjective *natural* is applied to a wine or its producer, it has been known to incite personal attacks and angry debates.

The notion of a "natural" wine is generally agreed to have started several decades ago, back in the 1960s, with a Beaujolais producer named Jules Chauvet. Mr. Chauvet was a chemist, *négociant*, and winemaker who lived from 1907 until 1989. He was an avowed champion of winemaking without pesticides, synthetic fertilizers, added sulfur, or cultured yeasts—and he inspired a number of winemakers to follow his lead.

These winemakers included rising star Beaujolais producers like Marcel Lapierre and Jean Foillard, who made wines that won attention and praise; gradually the natural wine philosophy began to spread outward to other parts of France—and eventually the rest of the world. There probably isn't a wine region today that doesn't have at least one self-proclaimed natural winemaker.

And that is perhaps the biggest problem with natural wine and winemakers: everything about it is self-proclaimed—and everyone has a different definition of what *natural* means. A natural wine isn't like an organic wine or a biodynamic wine, which are wines made according to specific practices and, in the case of organic wine, government certification. Natural wine is a much more elastic designation; there are no absolutes—or at least none that is officially sanctioned by anyone. Sometimes natural wine seems to be simply an individual interpretation of the facts.

Those facts include how the wine was made. If the wine was made in a manner that natural wine proponents deem "manipulative" (and that is the natural wine buzzword), it's called "unnatural" by its critics. But when and where does the manipulation begin—and end? And who gets to decide what fits the category?

Does manipulation start in the vineyard with the removal of a few green leaves (to promote berry growth) or with irrigation? If the ground is naturally dry, should the vines not be left to struggle? Is watering a kind of manipulation?

Or does the manipulation, or its absence, count only when the winemaker is actually in his winery, deciding whether or not to remove some alcohol or perhaps add some sugar (called "chaptalization"; it is legal in some places and not others). And what if the wine was a bit weedy and underripe? Should a winemaker just leave it in that natural, if rather unpleasant, state? And what about a wine that's particularly fragile? Should the winemaker add some sulfur to protect it from oxidation or just let it spoil?

Some have declared that a wine is natural if it has "nothing added and nothing taken away." This sounds very simple and very appealing—and it's definitely catchy. (Natural wine proponents are very good at sloganeering.) But what about the way the wines taste? Isn't that what's most important? And could the wine taste better if it weren't left to itself? (Never mind that no wine actually makes itself.)

The fact that I care about most when it comes to wine is pleasure, not naturalness. Is the wine well made and is it pleasurable to drink? If it can be done with minimal intervention, that's definitely best, but if the winemaker needs to nudge it along to taste better—or to prevent flaws (like adding a bit of sulfur to ensure it doesn't fall apart on the way to my house), then I am perfectly happy with that as well.

Arnaud Tronche, the managing partner of Racines NY, a wine bar and restaurant in New York (a favorite haunt of natural wine fans), has what I think is exactly the right attitude when it comes to natural wines: he features producers who make wines with care and attention. Some, he says, are natural, while others are "natural enough."

How's Your Palate?

ONE OF THE HIGHEST COMPLIMENTS that one oenophile can bestow upon another is to call him or her a "palate." That is, a person who knows the texture of a Cabernet versus that of a Merlot, who knows that a Trousseau isn't something a bride brings to her groom but a red grape from the Jura region of France, who can determine if a Bordeaux was from the 1989 or 1990 vintage. This person might be admiringly said to possess a palate—or to be called a "palate" him- or herself.

A "palate" is technically physical (the roof of the mouth, your taste buds, and your nose), but it also represents a certain level of vinous knowledge and sophistication and *je ne sais quoi*. It's something that wine drinkers work to develop and refine. There are even classes and seminars that explain how this is done.

For a regular wine drinker, this is very good news. If you don't have a palate, you can always acquire one. And there are just a few steps that you need to follow. The first is the easiest: look at the wine. This sounds quite easy, but it's something that most people don't do for more than a second or two. But if you pause and take note of the color, the clarity, and the viscosity (i.e., heavy or light?), you'll be doing something that only a palate does very often.

The next step is to start sniffing—take short and purposeful sniffs into the glass. No sniff should last very long—just a few seconds—and it should be enough to determine if the wine is good or flawed. And what does it smell like? Red fruit? Black fruit? Apples and spice or wet dogs and newspaper? (In these last two cases it might be corked.)

The third step is the most pleasurable: taste it. A taste of the wine, preferably swirled around your mouth, should (mostly) confirm what you've already seen and smelled, although it could also tell you about the wine's texture and the weight.

Then it's time for the full evaluation, which means putting all these disparate parts together. How does a wine stack up, quality-wise, to other similar wines? (A palate will have a seemingly inexhaustible supply of cross-referenced wines, which comes from tasting and reading—and remembering them all too, even if it's something as old-fashioned as keeping notes in a book.)

The one thing that a true palate will never do is misspell the word. I can't count how many times I've read someone mention that they know a person with a great "palette" or worse, a "pallet." Do they really mean to compliment someone on their paint holder or their resemblance to something that's handled by a forklift?

Orange Is the Old Black

SOMEDAY—IN THE NOT-TOO-DISTANT FUTURE, I hope—wine drinkers will look back on this period of time with a mixture of pity and awe. The awe will come from the fact that we have so many great wines from all over the world to choose from and the pity will be because, with such vinous bounty, there were still people who made—and drank—orange wine.

Perhaps you are the lucky reader who has never had to find out what orange wine is for yourself, or had a sommelier force one upon you, or perhaps by the time that you're reading this page, the orange wine craze will have faded away.

The orange wine movement began some twenty years ago (though it's actually a much older phenomenon). The modern creator is generally agreed to be Josko Gravner, a winemaker from the Friuli region that straddles Italy and Slovenia. Mr. Gravner once made conventional white wines, but grew bored and restless and decided sometime in the 1990s to go back to making "ancient" sorts of wines—that is, white wines that he macerated and fermented with their skins intact inside clay vessels.

The resulting "skin contact" wine looked less white than orange—and attracted the attention of wine professionals, especially sommeliers, as well as a number of admiring winemakers. Some of these winemakers, especially those in Georgia (the country, not the state), had been making their own "orange" wines for many years; others, in places like Long Island, decided to try their hand at their own versions.

Orange wines are unlike a white and unlike a red, although they are probably more like a red than a white. They're tannic and sometimes a little bitter depending on how long the skins have contact with the juice. Sommeliers love orange wines because they believe that orange wines can work with all kinds of food—and of course very few "regular wine" drinkers understand them—so they need sommeliers to explain them too.

The tannins in orange wines mean they can even stand up to heartier foods, even meat. In fact, many wine professionals treat orange wines like red wines and serve them at cellar temperature. Some have "orange wine" sections on their wine lists—which a few oenophiles have told me they thought meant the wines were infused with the fruit.

And yet the very characteristics that sommeliers tout as their virtues are all the things that I like the least. I like my white wines crisp and refreshing, not chewy- and tired-seeming, and my red (and white) wines fresh, not oxidized. This will—and has—marked me as unimaginative or worse, but I hope that when these wines one day fade from view it will mark me instead as "prescient."

Wine the Second Time

SOME WINE PROBLEMS ARE NOT ACTUAL PROBLEMS but merely dilemmas. Like the problem of leftover wine. What should you do with leftover wine? It's a question that I field pretty often—even if it's a problem I rarely have myself.

A wine that's leftover sounds so forlorn, a wine that no one quite had sufficient appetite or desire to consume. Was it because it just wasn't quite compelling or was it because the bottle was simply too much? And what's the right thing to do with what remains in the bottle to ensure that it will be "redisovered" another night?

Most people just stick the cork back in the bottle and put it aside— the kitchen counter is the most popular spot. Other drinkers, a tad more enlightened, will put the bottle in the refrigerator. This is always preferable, even for a red wine, as the chill protects the wine and keeps it from degrading as quickly. (You can keep a wine in the refrigerator for a few days, and even longer if the wine is bottled under a screwcap, which is almost airtight.)

Another technique is to transfer the wine from its regular-sized bottle to one that is smaller. This reduces the amount of oxygen in the bottle by increasing the ratio of wine to air. (Most leftover bottles of wine contain less than half the original contents.)

There are also contraptions that will pump nitrous gas into the bottle, thereby "covering" the wine with a blanket of protective gas. And if that actually sounds appealing to you, you don't need to read the rest of this essay.

I'm particularly fond of freezing the bottle when you can't finish it the next day (perhaps you're going away?). This is a trick that I learned from a (late) great wine writer many years ago and it preserves the wine remarkably well.

I know lots of people who think that the best use of leftover wine is to use it as a component in something else—such as sangria. But that seems a bit like making French toast with day-old bread. Salad dressing is another favorite I've often seen cited, and a glaze for a roast chicken is one of my favorite food-related solutions, but the one I practice most often is even simpler. I live in a neighborhood populated by wine drinkers. If I have at least half a bottle left over and the wine is good, I simply walk next door to one of my neighbors, who will happily finish the bottle. My leftover wine is only left over for a few minutes at most.

Consider the Cork

THE CORK—it's so small and yet so critical to wine in all phases of its life—past, present, and future. A mere few ounces of cork material stand between the well-being of a wine and its eventual end. Oxygen is the enemy of wine, after all, and the cork is responsible for keeping it out of the bottle—while ensuring, at the same time, that the contents won't spill out.

This has been true for a very long time; cork has been an important part of the wine world for many hundreds of years. And however flawed (a cork is far from infallible, but more on that anon), it's a decided improvement over previous closures. For example, the Romans once favored oil-soaked rags. (I wish I could access some six-hundred-year-old tasting notes to find out how wine under rags actually tasted.)

Cork is a natural and ecologically sound sort of closure; a cork tree is only stripped every nine years for its use, and this operation is never performed at a time when it would hurt the tree. (Who knew there was such a thing as a cork-stripping season?)

Cork does get tainted on occasion; this is what people are talking about when they describe a wine as "corked" or having "cork taint": the cork itself has been infected with a chemical compound with a long alpha-numerical name (2,4,6-trichloroanisole) that can make the wine taste dull at best and at worst like a damp basement or wet dog. This is often caused by someone washing the corks with a chlorine solution, although there are other causes as well. A corked wine isn't dangerous—the compound isn't fatal—just unpleasant.

A wine cork is remarkably pliable for something that's almost airtight. It's particularly impressive when it's used to close a bottle of Champagne. The Champagne cork is actually made up of various parts of cork for added strength. Although a popped Champagne cork blossoms to look like a fat mushroom, it actually starts out as a regular cylindrical shape like any wine cork. The mushroom shape is the result of bearing all that pressure in the bottle (there is as much as 90 pounds of pressure per square inch in a bottle of Champagne) and also the fact that the cork is placed only halfway into the bottle before it's anchored and covered with a wire cage of sorts.

The wires keep the cork from popping out—though *pop* may be too gentle a term for a closure that's under as much pressure as an inflated bus tire. *Explode* might be a better verb to describe what happens when a Champagne cork is pulled out of a bottle in a less than cautious manner. There is actually a question circulating on the Internet: "Can you be killed by a Champagne cork?" (The answer is a less than completely comforting "Probably not—although it could put your eye out.") Clearly there is quite a lot that a cork can accomplish, both bad and good.

An Airtight Argument

A COUNTRY THE SIZE OF NEW ZEALAND doesn't get many opportunities to influence the world. But there are two things from New Zealand that have actually had a clear global impact—men's rugby and Sauvignon Blanc.

But the third Kiwi accomplishment is something that fewer people are aware they owe to New Zealand: the use of screw caps. These metal caps that screw onto the neck of a bottle of wine have been embraced more completely and more passionately by New Zealand winemakers than by anyone else—and sooner, too. More than ten years ago, New Zealand winemakers were quite vociferous in their efforts to convert others to their cause.

The first time I visited New Zealand, around the time of the millennium, one of the very first questions I was asked had to do with screw caps. Was I for them or against them? Every winemaker wanted to know. It was like declaring a political party or a favorite band, except that it was much more important—and a lot more personal. Any hesitation to say yes was clearly considered betrayal.

Perhaps a bit of background would be of some help. The New Zealand Screwcap Initiative was created in 2001 and gained support slowly across the two islands, but now it's almost impossible to find a New Zealand wine—red or white—that isn't bottled under a screw cap instead of a cork.

Screw caps on wine bottles are actually nothing new. They've been around for over half a century—the French introduced them first—but they didn't catch on with quality winemakers until the past decade or so. In the earlier years, the wines under screw cap were almost always cheap. And the screw cap itself—and there were several types—wasn't exactly an attractive device. But the screw cap market began shifting in the 1990s as the screw cap itself improved and quality-minded producers in Australia, led by Jeffrey Grosset, chose screw caps over corks.

Mr. Grosset was actually ahead of the New Zealand winemakers, spearheading the Australian Screwcap Initiative in the Clare Valley, where his Grosset winery is located. He attracted some local followers, but it was the New Zealanders whom he really inspired.

Among the attractions of a screw cap versus cork that these winemakers cited was the absence of cork taint (from a chemical compound that is found in some corks) and sporadic oxidation (a cork will allow a small amount of air into the bottle, whereas a screw cap is airtight), and a reliable long-term seal. I can vouch—unscientifically—for all three. I've never had a corked screw cap wine (although a wine can also be corked because of a winery—but that's a long story), and I've found that a half-empty bottle of wine closed by a screw cap lasts much longer than a wine under cork.

The New Zealand winemakers were remarkably effective in their campaign, and in just over ten years since they sought a change, screw caps have not only become all but universal in New Zealand but have also gained acceptability all over the world—especially in countries like Germany, Austria, Australia, and the United States. Some of the best wines in all of these countries are bottled under screw cap.

Perhaps New Zealanders haven't received quite as much credit for their pioneering work with screw caps as their prowess with rugby balls and Sauvignon, but for the noncorked, nonoxidative wines in the world, we all have New Zealand to thank.

The California Divide

IF THERE WAS A WINE WORLD EQUIVALENT of a celebrity face off, nothing would be more heated than a Napa versus Sonoma match. These two side-by-side wine regions in California have long been locked in battle of differences—real and perceived.

Consider a few of the differences. Sonoma is quite big (1,600 square miles) and Napa is comparatively small (800 acres). Grape-wise, Napa is specialized, while Sonoma is generalized. In Napa it's almost all Cabernet, while Sonoma has just about everything else—Chardonnay, Pinot Noir, Zinfandel, Sauvignon Blanc—and Cabernet, too. Sonoma has lots of rich winery owners; Napa has even more.

Of course there are plenty of ways that the two are virtually the same. Hotels in both places are equally pricey—ditto their restaurants and their gift shops. And their highway traffic is equally maddening.

And what of the wineries? In Napa both the tasting room staff and the tourists are better dressed than the average American. Napa is all about the scene and showing off (for tourists, not natives), while Sonoma people tend to keep a lower profile. Maybe that's why Napa residents travel to Sonoma if they want to "sin," as I was once told by a resident of Healdsburg, Sonoma. (She said this when we saw a famous winemaker dining in Sonoma with a woman who was not his wife.)

Both Napa and Sonoma had larger-than-life heroes: Napa's was Robert Mondavi, who created his own version of a wine Disneyland and put Napa on the world map. Sonoma had Jess Jackson, whose Sonoma-based Kendall-Jackson winery put Chardonnay in just about every American's glass.

Of all their differences, perhaps the greatest between Napa and Sonoma are their terroirs—their topography, climate, elevation, and soil. Where Sonoma shoulders up to the ocean as well as the mountains, the redwoods, and the hills, Napa is effectively landlocked. (Though it does have a rather nice, rather large lake, which tourists rarely seem to visit.)

Napa has dramatic mountain ranges with American Indian names —like the Mayacamas Mountain range, the Vaca mountain range, and all the various mountain AVAs (official growing regions) like Spring Mountain, Mount Veeder, and Diamond Mountain. Everyone in Napa wants a vineyard on a mountain although since it's Napa, I'd bet they'd rather own the mountain itself.

Perhaps the biggest difference between Napa and Sonoma is the amount of time they spend talking about one another. Sonoma people like to explain why they are "not like Napa," whereas Napa residents never see much of a reason to mention Sonoma.

Form and Function

OENOPHILES LIKE TO DEBATE the right type of corkscrew the way that chefs like to argue about the right kitchen knives. A basic yet critical tool of the trade, the corkscrew has a very simple design, although its many interpretations can be quite complex.

I own about a dozen corkscrews but there is one that I use over and over again: a simple waiter's corkscrew made by Laguiole, a French company that makes terrific knives as well. Their handmade corkscrews that cost hundreds of dollars are considered the best, although they have cheaper iterations as well. The waiter's corkscrew, also known as the waiter's friend, is the standard corkscrew that you see in most restaurants. Small enough to fit in a (waiter's) pocket, it generally comes equipped with three things: a knife to cut the foil, a worm to pierce the cork, and a lever to pull it out of the bottle. A waiter's corkscrew is vastly superior to the nutcracker-type corkscrew that tends to tear up corks and that far too many people I know happen to use.

Maybe the biggest relatively recent corkscrew invention is the Rabbit—aka the Black Rabbit Wine Opener. *Contraption* is the (cranky) word I'd employ to describe the bulky, heavy black tool that looks more like a stapling gun than something made to extract a cork. The Rabbit's creators claim that their tool can "pull a cork out of a bottle in three seconds flat," as if speed were the be-all and end-all of opening a bottle of wine. It may be efficient, but it's certainly not very attractive or, for that matter, ceremonial.

The right sort of corkscrew does more than simply open a bottle; it gives the sort of satisfaction to its user that can only be experienced by wielding a well-made instrument of any kind. The difference between a hand-crafted corkscrew and a cheap one—or a heavy-duty contraption—is the difference between driving a Maserati and a truck. They will both get you where you are going, but only one will accomplish it in great style.

Room to Drink

AT ONE TIME OR ANOTHER just about every wine drinker will eventually visit a winery tasting room. It's practically a rite of passage for serious and casual drinkers alike. It's also a ritual that I don't understand. For starters, lots of the people I've met in tasting rooms (which should really be called drinking rooms, by the way) have had the wines from the winery they're visiting many times before. They're tasting—or rather, drinking—what they've had before but in much, much smaller amounts, but this time they aren't sitting comfortably at home but standing up at a bar.

I actually once watched a woman buy a case of white Zinfandel in the Beringer Vineyards tasting room years ago. (Their tasting room was definitely a drinking room.) As anyone who has ever bought wine in a grocery store knows, Beringer white Zinfandel is one of the most ubiquitous wines in the world. And yet, it was the wine that this particular tasting room visitor wanted to buy.

Another slightly disconcerting possibility of the tasting room experience is that the person standing behind the counter may actually know very little about wine. He or she is only expected to memorize a few facts about the winery's offerings and to make sure not to give a too-generous pour. General wine questions often leave such workers slightly flummoxed. They only know the facts they're supposed to recite—like how long the winery's reserve Merlot spent in the barrel or where the Chardonnay vineyard is located. But don't think to ask what exactly takes place during malolactic fermentation or if the Cabernet grape originated in Argentina or France.

But wine isn't often the main point—at least not in terms of merchandise—at a certain sort of commercial tasting room, in fact, the wine bottles are often outnumbered by the T-shirts, the snacks, the glassware, and the commemorative hats. Most winery tasting rooms look more like airport gift shops than places where wine is meant to be discussed and consumed. (Smaller and/or more sophisticated wineries often forgo the merchandise altogether and just sell the wine.)

The winery tasting room that was the best example of merchandising at the fore was the old Francis Ford Coppola Rubicon Estate in Napa, where people could buy trinkets related—and unrelated—to his movies. Mostly it was just stuff that Mr. Coppola liked—or that his buying teams liked; he actually employed scouts to find really cool stuff. Several years ago he moved all the movie memorabilia and the toys and the stuff to his winery in Sonoma because he didn't want the focus to be taken away from the wine. Or at least not a "serious" wine like Rubicon.

On the other hand, I know that wine is expensive to produce and that vineyards are even more expensive to maintain. And just as wine and liquor help to subsidize the cost of elaborate food in restaurants so too do hats and stuffed animals help pay for the cost of fixing the bottling line or replanting a row of Chardonnay. That's one reason why I will occasionally buy my husband yet another (insert winery logo) baseball hat.

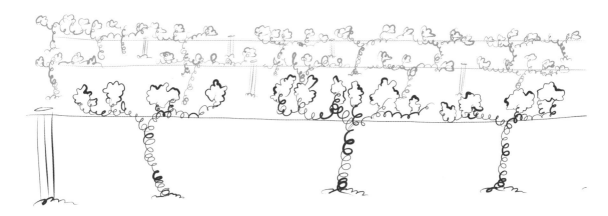

Tough Times, Good Wines

ADVERSITY BUILDS CHARACTER; it's a saying that applies as much to grapevines as it does to individuals. Vines need to struggle, winemakers say—almost as often as they like to proclaim that their "wines are made in the vineyard" (this is my favorite faux-modest cliché). Another favorite saying captures this perhaps even more vividly: "A scrawny vine makes a great wine."

A vine that doesn't have to work hard will create an innocuous wine—much in the same way that a life of leisure may produce a ne'er-do-well. When a vine struggles, it reaches deep into the soil to obtain the needed nutrients. If the soil was rich and the nutrients were plentiful, the vine would put its energy into the leaves and the plant and not the fruit. But when resources (water and nutrients) are few the vine's roots are forced to dig deeper, work harder. This turns out to be particularly useful when the conditions are dire—for example, when there is too little rain. Because the roots run deep they can reach the water.

Limited access to water can produce smaller, more vivid, more intense-tasting fruit (the smaller the grape, the less water inside). A closely spaced vineyard also has a stressful effect: it forces the vines to compete for nutrients and it also reduces the vigor of the canopy—that's the viticultural term for the leaves of the vine. The same is true, by the way, of a vine planted on a steep rocky slope; it will struggle as well in a marginal soil.

Of course, stress isn't always a boon and it can also do real damage—to people and vines alike. The stress of a prolonged and too-cold winter, a long bout of hail right near harvest, or day after day of a pounding, ceaseless rain or, for that matter, months of drought can all take their toll—and can ultimately even destroy the vines.

Everything has to be done at the right time and in the right proportion: water has to be apportioned or applied (through irrigation) at specific times, the extraneous fruit has to be removed early in the growing season (called a green harvest), and perhaps the too-sheltering leaves have to be stripped away (thereby preventing rot and helping the fruit to ripen properly). These are a few widely accepted viticultural practices that are called—in words that a business executive would appreciate—the "stress management" of a vine.

Adventurous Spirits

WHETHER OR NOT WINEMAKING is a particularly heroic business (worthwhile, yes; heroic probably not), I have many winemaking heroes. They're the mavericks who tilt against windmills, strive against terrible odds, tackle seemingly impossible projects or grapes, and emerge—if not always triumphant—then at least undeterred.

These mavericks all have one thing in common: what former President George H. W. Bush once called "the vision thing." While their vision was often underwritten by money (it's the wine business, after all), it was also informed by madness.

I could name dozens and dozens of winemakers deserving of hero status, but to keep this story to a manageable length I'll focus on just four whom I truly admire. Two already hold a place in winemaking history; the other two are still earning theirs.

My two early wine heroes, Martin Ray and Dr. Konstantin Frank, have both passed away, but they left an indisputable mark on wine to this day (and were considered by many to be a bit crazy).

My two present-day heroes have never been considered madmen as far as I know, but Bill Harlan of Harlan Estate in Napa Valley and Russell McCall of Long Island have their own quixotic visions as well.

Dr. Konstantin Frank

Dr. Frank, a Russian émigré living in upstate New York, believed that Riesling could be successfully grown in the Finger Lakes. He proposed this to various people back in the 1950s while he was working menial jobs, including one sweeping floors at Cornell University. His employer and the local winemakers took exception to the idea, insisting that only the hardy hybrids (non-noble grapes) could survive the harsh winters of upstate New York. At a wine conference, he shared his ideas with Charles Fournier of Gold Seal, a large wine producer. Fournier hired him on the spot and made him Director of Research at Gold Seal. It turned out that not only was Dr. Frank right, but he helped to create an entire wine industry based on great Finger Lakes Rieslings—and nobody talks about hybrids today.

Martin Ray

Around the same time that Dr. Frank was championing Riesling, Martin Ray, a winemaker from California, was pushing his own unpopular causes, like eschewing wine made with additives and promoting the accurate labeling of wines. Back in those days, a wine could be labeled Chardonnay and yet actually contain up to 49 percent of some other grape. Mr. Ray produced some notable wines at his winery in Santa Cruz, and although he went broke (not all mavericks are great businessmen), his Chardonnays and Pinot Noirs are still considered touchstones for California winemakers today.

Bill Harlan

Bill Harlan was a millionaire, not a madman, when he founded Harlan Estate in 1984. Mr. Harlan made his money in many non-wine ventures, most notably real estate (he started the famous and fabulous Meadowood Resort), and when it came to wine he had a specific goal: he wanted to make a wine that would be considered a "first growth," aka grand cru—equal to Bordeaux first growth, Lafite, Mouton, and Latour.

Mr. Harlan's sanity was probably questioned more than a few times over the years—particularly when he chose to plant vineyards high above the valley floor. Although hillside vineyards are championed today, they were regarded as a rather radical place to plant grapes when Bill Harlan began his work.

The Harlan Estate red is now one of the most expensive wines in the Napa Valley—and has earned the sobriquet "cult Cabernet" (a kind of American version of a first growth). And while the prestige of the cult Cab designation has faded a bit in recent years, Harlan Estate's place in California wine history is almost assured.

Russell McCall

It's unlikely that Long Island will ever be home to a wine that could be described by the word *cult*, but Russell McCall, successful Atlanta businessman and polo player turned farmer and vintner on the North Fork, is making remarkably good Pinot Noir on eastern Long Island against all the odds.

The Long Island climate (humid and damp) isn't regarded as one suitable to the temperamental and fragile grape, and no one else had tried their hand at growing it in a serious way with any success, but Mr. McCall, an avowed Pinotphile, was convinced he had the right exposition and land. He developed the largest Pinot Noir vineyard on Long Island and has the wines made upstate at Millbrook Winery, whose proprietor, John Dyson, just happens to own Williams Selyem, one of California's most famous Pinot Noir estates.

Dr. Frank's and Martin Ray's visions have long since been realized, and Bill Harlan has provided a blueprint for those who also aspire to great wine—he started an elite winemaking club called the Napa Valley Reserve. Meanwhile, Russell McCall has yet to inspire many other producers to follow him down the Pinot Noir path and ten years from now, his investment may seem foolhardy—or it may seem wise. But all of these men gambled on the possibility of fortune or failure. No one becomes a hero, after all, by playing it safe.

The Pleasures of Pouring

THERE'S SOMETHING QUITE WORLDLY AND POLISHED, per-haps even erudite, about decanting a bottle of wine. The simple act of pouring wine from a bottle into some sort of stylish receptacle seems to elevate both wine and wine drinker. And the receptacle doesn't have to be anything special—it doesn't need to be made from fancy crystal or cut glass—even a large water pitcher will do. The motion of the wine provides all the color, the beauty, and the drama of the moment.

The main reason to decant a wine is entirely practical: it makes the wine more pleasurable to drink. Pouring the wine from bottle to decanter aerates (oxygenates) the wine, making its aromas more pronounced. A decanted wine will almost always have more vivid aromas than one that is poured directly from the bottle. A wine that is decanted is also softer, more approachable, for the same reasons; the oxygen breaks the tannin chain too. A couple of hours in a decanter can make a tannic wine much more approachable than it would be if it were poured right from the bottle.

A wine is also decanted if it's older and possessed of a sediment (the stuff that collects at the bottom of a bottle) that would otherwise end up in somebody's glass. Wines with a lot of sediment are almost exclusively red wines with a lot of structure and a fair amount of tannin; Cabernet-based wines are chief candidates for decanting. This is rarely the reason to decant a young wine, as wines don't usually "throw" much sediment in their youth. (Yes, that is the verb that wine professionals use to describe the act of dislodging the stuff.)

The first type of decanting can be done in a pretty straightforward manner: open the bottle and pour it out into the receptacle. The second type of decanting must be done more carefully, lest you end up pouring the sediment into the glass with the wine. This second type of decanting must be done slowly, carefully, even ceremoniously. Some sommeliers like to add a bit more to the majesty of the occasion by pouring the bottle from a straw cradle of sorts (to steady the bottle and presumably their hands) into the decanter. They might even pour the wine out over the light of a single

candle (to keep an eye on the sediment), although the presence of flame might only increase the danger quotient for a wine amateur.

I decant wines more often for the first reason—to increase their aromatic appeal and make them a bit softer—than the second, but I drink most of my wines fairly young. And while I have several very nice decanters (all presents), I've been known to use a large flower vase in a pinch, which is fun but perhaps a bit awkward to pour.

I've rarely decanted a non-red wine, although there was a wine director at a restaurant in the Napa Valley who liked to decant every wine that she poured—not just the obvious stuff like a big Napa Valley Cabernet or young red Bordeaux but wines like Pinot Grigio and Prosecco, too. I thought at the time that this was taking decanting a bit far. When is the last time you drank a glass of decanted Prosecco? On the other hand, she decanted with such joy and abandon it was hard not to enjoy the moment—and her performance. Decanting can also be performance art.

The Pinot Effect

ALTHOUGH PINOT NOIR has been cultivated for centuries, it took a certain American movie to make Pinot Noir officially "hot." Or at least that's the explanation I've been hearing since 2004. That's the year that *Sideways* debuted—the movie whose hero, Miles, famously delivers a very long and very passionate speech about Pinot Noir.

When asked why he loves Pinot Noir so much, this is what Miles (played by Paul Giamatti) replies: "It's not a survivor like Cabernet, which can just grow anywhere and, uh, thrive even when it's neglected. No, Pinot needs constant care and attention. You know? And in fact it can only grow in these really specific, little, tucked-away corners of the world. And—and only the most patient and nurturing of growers can do it, really. Only somebody who really takes the time to understand Pinot's potential can then coax it into its fullest expression. Then, I mean, oh its flavors, they're just the most haunting and brilliant and thrilling and subtle and . . . ancient on the planet."

Never mind he's actually talking about himself, Miles is the one who is (still) most often credited as the one responsible for making non-Pinot drinkers suddenly desperate to drink the stuff. (And to simultaneously eschew Merlot, since Miles is as anti-Merlot as he is pro-Pinot.)

But if *Sideways* were really the reason, would its fans still be so intensely passionate about Pinot Noir ten years after the fact? Would planting (and sales) still be ascending? I tend to think not, especially since other grapes have cycled in and out of fashion in just a matter of a few years—or even less. Does anyone remember the minute or two that Syrah was fashionable or, for that matter, Merlot?

The great virtue of Pinot Noir is approachability. From its soft, pliant nature to its perfumed aromas of red berry fruit and ability to fit most any food, Pinot Noir is easy to say and easy to drink. It's a wine that someone as disaffected (and disliked) as Miles would want to resemble.

And, of course, the Pinot Noir speech worked a small movie miracle and made Miles—an unsympathetic, small-minded petty thief (does anyone besides me recall that Miles actually stole money from his mother?) into a hero—one who got the girl in the end.

Even Paul Giamatti had a different take than the popular belief about his character. In an interview on Toronto television, he said this of Miles: "He has this whole pretentious thing about wine that's really just to cover up the fact he's a drunk." Pinot lovers should consider finding a new hero to further their cause.

Aperitif, Anyone?

"THIS IS A GREAT APERITIF WINE," a friend remarked when I served her a glass of a light-bodied red. My initial response was to regard her comment as a criticism. After all, an aperitif wine isn't serious or important and it's often cheap.

I immediately noted the price—aloud. "This wine cost thirty-five dollars," I said, knowing that my friends were devoted followers of the cheap aperitif rule. (Champagne is their single, infrequent exception.) My friend claimed she didn't mean to slander my wine. "I love it," she said reassuringly. "I would pay thirty-five dollars for it too."

This exchange made me consider what qualities are essential in a great aperitif wine, and I came up with a few fast (but not hard) rules:

An aperitif wine must be refreshing. It must invigorate and enliven the palate. It must have enough character and interest to make an impression—but not too much. A great aperitif wine is a whisper, not a shout.

An aperitif wine should be fairly light bodied and fairly high in acidity. That's why Champagne works so well—it has lots of acidity. A Blanc de Blancs Champagne (a Champagne made entirely from Chardonnay) is a perfect aperitif, though most any Champagne or dry sparkling wine will do. Ditto a Rosé that's light and lively (nothing too darkly colored). A wine with acidity whets the palate and prepares the wine drinker for what is to come.

An aperitif wine should be low in alcohol. This is a particularly crucial characteristic considering that more—and more—wine is likely to be served with the meal. Check the alcohol content on the label. An aperitif wine should be under 12 percent—and there are wines like Vinho Verde, the white wine from Portugal, and many German Rieslings that are even lower (from 7 to 11 percent).

There are some lower-alcohol, high-acidity red wines from the Alto Adige region of Italy made from grapes with challenging names like Lagrein and Schiava, and a fragrant red from the Lacrima grape in the country's Marche region. The Italians are particularly talented at the art of aperitivo—which is as much a lifestyle for Italians as it is a predinner drink. Pinot Grigio is a perfect, if slightly underwhelming, aperitif wine.

The French, who contributed the word *apéritif* to our vocabulary, are also, unsurprisingly, the source of some very good aperitif wines—both white and red—as well as some classic aperitifs like Lillet and Vermouth. Aside from the aforementioned Champagne, the wines of the Loire Valley are almost universally aperitif appropriate—from well-known wine districts like Sancerre and Muscadet to lesser-known areas like Chinon, Saumur, and Bourgueil.

There aren't as many American wines that are aperitif appropriate—perhaps because our collective preference is for wines with more fruit, more power, and more flavor. And an aperitif wine is, above all, about subtlety and finesse and (occasionally) price.

Too Much Sharing

WINE IS A SOCIAL BEVERAGE MEANT TO BE SHARED. But does that principle apply to everything related to wine—photos and labels and tasting notes as well? Should all memorable bottles and meals be immediately downloaded to Facebook and Twitter and Instagram, not to mention wine apps like Delectable and Vivino?

Social media presents twin opportunities for oenophiles, equally weighted: to learn something about wine or to brag about the wine you just had. Do you want to know what thirty or forty perfect strangers think of the wine you just tasted? Or do you want thirty or forty of those very same people to know what you just consumed (and how much you paid for it)?

I find some social media tools extremely useful; Delectable is fun, and certain wine professionals have truly informative Twitter feeds (and not just pictures of bottles). These can be good sources of new wines and obscure but interesting producers, but they can also be quite distracting. So much information to digest in so little time!

And, quite frankly, they can also be depressing. There are always lots of well-heeled people and top sommeliers who are drinking more and better than I ever have in my life. Maybe there should be a special app called Wine Envy, since that's what a lot of these tools—and their users—seem to (are intended to?) inspire.

Of course, that's not what social media mavens say is their intention. Instead, they like to focus on their role in "democratizing" wine. They use the "d" word quite often—as if there were some sort of wine autocrat blocking the way of would-be wine lovers. Wine is too complicated, too demanding, and too dependent on wine critics and wine professionals, they say—but that's also what makes wines special and interesting. If wine weren't so complicated, all those wine app users wouldn't have much to say.

This insistence that wine needs to made more "democratic" is something I'm not convinced is true—or for that matter necessary. Crowdsourcing just means you have access to a lot more opinions (like the wine drinker who thinks Smoking Loon Pinot Noir is one of the best wines in the world), but not necessarily more good information. (Smoking Loon is a nine-dollar wine sold in grocery stores. What's more democratic than being able to buy a bottle of Pinot Noir along with your steak?)

I guess I will always be a little conflicted when it comes to social media tools. Can they expand your appreciation of wine and broaden your knowledge or do they exist simply to give your ego a boost? As Frank Sinatra once said in a song, "It all depends on you."

Critical Attention

WHAT IS A WINE CRITIC? It's a question that is probably posed a lot less often by regular wine drinkers than it probably is by the wine critics themselves. Most wine drinkers only know of a critic's existence by means of a numerical score hanging from tag on a bottle in a store. A wine critic is someone whose advice (or numbers) you can trust.

But how did that wine critic become someone whose opinion is worthy of note, let alone one that moves bottles off the store shelves? The famous American wine critic Robert M. Parker, Jr., posited that he became a critic the same way anyone else could have—with a pen, a notebook, and a few bottles of wine.

It's a folksy half truth; the world's most powerful voice in wine rose to prominence in a more methodical way. First he created a regional wine newsletter at a time when there were few such publications, and he awarded scores like the ones schoolchildren receive—on a scale from 50 to 100 points. Many would-be critics followed suit.

But there are many other methods of marking a wine. Some use glasses (the Italians' highest mark comes in the form of three-glass salute, aka the *tre bicchieri*); and some employ a system of "puffs," which look a bit like marshmallows: five puffs is the top score. A lot of British wine writers favor a 20-point system whereby wines are rated on a scale from 10 to 20 points. This is a system that hasn't resonated at all on American shores, perhaps because we don't know that a 17-point wine is actually pretty good.

Wine critics rating tangible and intangible facts about a wine and how it measures against a particular type (for example, a Bordeaux wine should taste, smell, and appear like a Bordeaux, not a Burgundy or a wine from the Rhône) The tangible facts about a wine are elements that include its aroma, its balance, and its persistence in the mouth. The intangibles tend to be more emotional—the kind of reaction that the wine elicits.

One upon a time, wine critics were actually involved in the wine business. Mr. Parker was the first wine critic of note who had no ties to the wine trade, and he made much of that fact, claiming he was beholden to no one and so would deliver impartial advice. Prior to Mr. Parker's rise in the 1980s, the critics and wine writers that anyone paid attention to (and there really weren't many) were in the wine business themselves.

This was especially true of English wine writers decades ago (and still today) who were wine merchants who became writers and sometimes held both jobs simultaneously. I visited a wine producer in Spain many years ago who told me about a certain English wine writer who had visited the week before—and filled the trunk of his car with free wine samples before he left.

Loading free cases of wine into a car isn't something a credible critic would do, of course. There are things that wine critics should and should not do—or know. I actually found a website that offers (anonymous) counsel for would-be wine critics. They should learn how to identify grapes and perhaps take a course in winemaking, advises the site. This made sense. Knowledge is never a bad thing for a wine drinker, much less a wine critic, to have—although the same site counseled getting "a degree in wine." (There isn't really such a degree. You can't graduate with a B.A. in "wine" the way you can have one in, say, English.)

The site also instructed would-be critics to just start writing. (The actual words were "get the pen flowing"; apparently would-be critics are not put off by clichés.) While aspiring critics should have opinions (and scores) in order to truly distinguish themselves and to attract readers, they also need, of course, words.

The best critic is someone whose descriptions are accurate and reliable and ultimately whose taste aligns with your own.

The World's Classiest Grape

CABERNET SAUVIGNON IS THE WORLD'S CLASSIEST GRAPE. Whether or not that's actually true, it's what many wine drinkers seem to believe. Want to give someone a gift bottle but don't know them well? Cabernet Sauvignon is the safest and easiest way to look good. And if you're a winemaker who wants to charge a lot of money for a wine, what other grape would you possibly choose? The price of a good Cabernet Sauvignon will (almost) always be more than a similar-caliber Cabernet Franc or Merlot.

From its perfectly balanced two-part name to the famous places where it is found (Bordeaux and Napa), Cabernet Sauvignon confers a kind of instant cachet upon both producer and place—more than any other grape, even its Burgundian counterparts, Pinot Noir and Chardonnay. I have a few theories as to why this is true.

One reason may be the grape itself. Cabernet is extremely reliable and widely grown—it's translatable to a wide variety of soils and wine-drinking cultures. While Bordeaux and Napa may get most of the attention and the acclaim (and the money, of course) for their Cabernets, it's actually grown in a wide range of places—from Argentina to New Zealand to Italy and many countries in between. Cabernet has fan club members all over the world.

Cabernet is also possessed of just the right balance of structure and fruit to be appealing to drink young but serious enough to age gracefully for years, even decades (depending on the place where the wine is made as well as its style). The best Cabernets are some of the most age-worthy wines in the world. Cabernet is also a grape that appeals to both genders—unlike, say, Pinot Grigio. The name can be shortened to a manly-sounding "Cab," and women can feel empowered by saying it too. Perhaps that would be a great slogan (Cabernet is the kind of grape that seems to warrant a slogan). Cabernet Sauvignon: a manly grape—that women like too.

Five Essential Wine Words

A SMALL DICTIONARY COULD BE CREATED of wine-tasting terms. There are veritable orchards and fields full of fruits (strawberries, cherries, blackberries, lemons, oranges, melons, and the occasional kiwi). And there are words that might be otherwise utilized to seduce (supple, silky, fragrant) and words for flavor, texture, and appearance. There are multiple gradations of sweet and dry. But what are the words that are truly essential? I've narrowed it to five. They may or may not help you to understand wine better, but they'll make it sound as if you do.

Acidity

All wines—red, white, or rosé—must have some amount of acidity. This acts as both a preservative and framework for a wine. Some wines have more acidity than others, depending on the grape, the growing region, and the winemaking technique; think of it as a pucker factor from one to ten, with New Zealand Sauvignon Blanc near ten and a California Zinfandel much closer to one.

Acidity occurs naturally in wine, although it may be added during winemaking as well. There are various types of acidity: malic, citric, and lactic acid. Each contributes a different component to the wine.

The words used to describe acidity are generally friendly ones like *crisp* and *bright* and *clean* and *lively*. You never, ever say "acidic" unless the acidity is more prominent than anything else, because that's an undesirable word—as I remind many of my friends when they pronounce a wine "acidic" in an often unwitting insult.

Aroma

The most important aspect of a wine is its aroma. The famous French oenologist Émile Peynaud is often credited as the man who said "aroma is what gives wine its personality." Other winemaking experts have proclaimed that it contributed 80 percent to the character of a wine. Without an aroma, wine, just like food, offers a pretty limited palate of possibilities; there's texture and temperature and length, but not much else to say without an aroma. A lot of wine drinkers mistake aroma descriptions as words for flavors—like berries and spice and earth—but in fact they're not something you could detect by tasting: try holding your nose the next time you're drinking a wine and you'll see.

Balance

When everything is in harmony it's defined as being in balance—in wine and in life. Of course, balance is every bit as much an elusive goal in wine as it is in anything else, and a wine that is truly well balanced, that isn't "too" much of anything—"too oaky" or "too high in acidity" or "too light" or "too dark"—is a rare find. Balance is when nothing sticks out—when there isn't a surfeit or an insufficiency of any one component. It's also become something of a marketing term: there is a group of wine professionals who promote "wines in balance" but actually mean wines below 14.2 percent alcohol. Of course, if a wine were really in balance, its alcohol level would be immaterial because it would not be noticeable.

Structure

Like a building or a car, a wine has components that hold it together. One of those components is acidity, another is tannin, and another is alcohol. Without sufficient quantities of each, the wine will fall apart. It will taste flabby and characterless. Imagine what a flat soda tastes like. That's what a wine without structure resembles. A wine's structure also determines its size: Is it a big wine or one that's small bodied? Size matters when it comes to matching a wine with food, and when it comes to its ability to last through time. A big wine might be less versatile, but it might last longer.

Texture

The way a wine feels in the mouth has everything to do with its texture. A wine-tasting term (that I'm admittedly not overly fond of) is *mouth-feel*. When someone describes the mouthfeel, they're talking about texture. There are wines that are rich and opulent, "mouth coating," there are wines that are lean or thin, and there are wines that are supple and succulent.

The components that contribute to texture are the same components that create its structure: the alcohol, tannins, and acidity. They are all interconnected. The weight of a wine is described in words that describe texture, such as *chewy* or *dense* or even *rustic*. But there is one commonly used texture word that a retailer once told me was the most meaningless word of all: *smooth*. One person's smooth could be another person's rough. As a wine descriptor, he said, it means nothing at all.

Some Like It Tart

IT ALL STARTED IN NEW ZEALAND. A white wine made on that small and faraway set of islands turned out to be one of the best-selling wines of our time. The year was 1985 and the wine was Cloudy Bay Sauvignon Blanc. It was a perfect name and, as it turned out, a perfect ambassador for a grape that no one up to that point had thought much about.

There had certainly been Sauvignon Blanc in this country before Cloudy Bay; there were French Sauvignon Blancs like Pouilly-Fumé and Sancerre, and there was plenty of Sauvignon Blanc grown in California, too. And yet California winemakers didn't really seem to know what to do with the grape—often treating it as a sort of lesser Chardonnay, squashed under loads of oak—and few wine drinkers probably knew that Sancerre was (also) Sauvignon Blanc.

The late Napa vintner and vinous shaman Robert Mondavi was the first and most famous proponent of this particular style—which he cleverly called "Fumé Blanc." This was a quintessentially American amalgamation of two French words—*blanc* (white) and *Fumé*, a reference to the Pouilly-Fumé region of the Loire Valley. But even Mondavi couldn't make Sauvignon Blanc popular—at least not the way that Cloudy Bay did.

The New Zealand superstar introduced Americans to a totally different style of white wine—a wine with a bracing acidity, raciness, and verve. In fact, when the word *racy* was first applied to a wine, it was probably with regard to Cloudy Bay. The wine, with its half-moody, half-boring label (undulating gray and white), sold out immediately—and inspired dozens if not hundreds of imitations from all over New Zealand and the rest of the world. Even French winemakers took to calling their Sancerres "New Zealand" style. (This was arguably the greatest accomplishment of all for New Zealand Sauvignon Blanc.)

Kiwi-made Sauvignons ignited a passion for the grape among wine drinkers who were looking for something leaner and juicier and, well, chic-er than tried and true Chardonnay. Among certain women I know, a lean style was somehow equated with a leaner physique or, in some cases, great finesse.

There are now acceptable, if not sought-after Sauvignon Blancs made all over the world—Chile, for example, makes very good examples that have the added virtue of being very cheap. Sauvignon Blancs from producers like Casa Lapostolle and Casa Marin are always good bets. It's also made wines from otherwise hard-to-market regions like Long Island easier to sell. (There happen to be some very good Sauvignon Blancs made there as well by producers like Paumanok, Jamesport, and Macari Vineyards.)

In fact, I think a case study should be made of how one brand and one grape was able to turn an entire winemaking industry on its head— and inspire a passion that shows no sign of abating. An English wine merchant once described Cloudy Bay as having "middle-class cachet," and while he meant that in a derogatory fashion, I find it cheering. Middle-class drinkers buy most of the world's wines.

A Fluid Profession

I ONCE RECEIVED A NOTE FROM A READER of my *Wall Street Journal* column who had encountered a sommelier in a retail wine store and was quite confused. "I thought sommeliers worked in restaurants," he wrote. "Could he actually have been a real sommelier?" he asked, thinking perhaps there was some rogue merchant on the loose.

I explained to this reader that many wine educators and wine writers actually called themselves sommeliers although they had never been anywhere near a table of customers as far as I knew. I also admitted that I too was confused by the profligate use of the word. After all, the exact definition of the sommelier job is a "wine waiter." Was it fair to the real, working wine waiters that so many nonpros had appropriated their title—if not their actual job?

I put the question to Bernie Sun, a former top New York sommelier and former corporate beverage director of the Jean-Georges Vongerichten restaurant group based in New York. Didn't he think that their use was wrong?

But Mr. Sun, an affable fellow, didn't actually share my outrage over the annexation; in fact he said he was "okay" with the use of the title by nonsoms, even though "technically a sommelier works in a restaurant and serves wine." But since so many titles were so readily bandied about these days, Mr. Sun didn't have a problem with a retailer making use of it. After all, someone working retail was serving wine too—albeit in a different way, reasoned the generous-minded Mr. Sun.

But why did they take the title at all? Perhaps the appropriation has to do with the recent glamorization of the job—and sommeliers are seen as rather glamorous these days. More and more "soms" (as they call themselves) are showing up in fashion spreads in magazines and on reality shows on TV. They're turning into ersatz celebrity chefs, albeit with (far) fewer tools.

But what do they do to earn their fame? Once more I turned to Mr. Sun for an answer. What did he think was necessary to be a sommelier today? Passion for wine and passion for people were important, he replied. Passion was particularly important because there wasn't a lot of money in the job. "If you add up how much we work and how much we make it's probably about three dollars an hour," Mr. Sun told me. (A starting sommelier may make less than forty thousand dollars a year.) That certainly didn't sound glamorous—nor did the other duties that Mr. Sun outlined as a necessary part of the job—like stacking boxes and tracking purchases on Excel spreadsheets. The last part was key; as Mr. Sun pointed out, a sommelier had to make money for the restaurant. Or, as Mr. Sun put it: "A sommelier is a revenue center." (Mr. Sun, however affable, doesn't mince words or sugarcoat facts.)

Of course, those revenue centers get to taste lots of good wine and wear some very nice suits. Sommeliers are invariably well turned out, save perhaps for their footware. Sommeliers' shoes are definitely the unglamorous kind. But then these revenue centers spend lots of time on their feet, running from the cellar to the restaurant floor. The practical facts of sommelier footwear was something that impressed me the most when I spent time shadowing some great sommeliers years ago. They weren't only articulate, affable, and deeply wine-knowledgeable, they were forever in motion. In fact, that may be the one reason why most sommeliers eventually leave the business after a certain age: it's not only an all-consuming position but a physical ordeal as well. And at a certain age and a certain point a sommelier will probably just want to sit down.

Seasonal Disorder

ONE OF THE WINE WORLD'S MOST SUCCESSFUL INVENTIONS isn't the wine glass, the decanter, or even the corkscrew, but the so-called "seasonal wine." Touted by wine merchants and sommeliers and, yes, far too many wine journalists too, a seasonal wine is one that is theoretically meant to be consumed at certain times of the year. There are seasonal reds and seasonal whites and every single Rosé ever made is somehow regarded as only a seasonal wine. It's the color that gets the shortest shrift, seasonally speaking.

Rosé is considered such a seasonal specialty that it can be quite hard to find a bottle of the stuff in, say, mid-November, or for that matter, a week after Labor Day in certain stores. Importers and distributors of Rosé have told me that some retailers have flat-out refused to buy Rosé. These merchants are afraid they will get stuck with the wines after that all-important day in early September. Never mind that it may be just as hot in September as it was when they were guzzling gallons of the pink stuff in July.

And Rosé pairs nicely with all kinds of dishes—from fish to chicken and the inevitable pasta—in other words, with the kind of food that people don't eat only in summer but throughout the year. Rosé has the juiciness of a white wine and the body of a light red. And it's such a cheery color. Why wouldn't someone want a bottle of it to brighten a January day? It might help to dispel some of that seasonal gloom.

White wine is, of course, at its gustatory pinnacle between April and August (and at art openings just about any time of the year). There are quite a few "seasonal" whites that can be hard to find in the colder months of the year. I'm thinking of Muscadets from the Loire Valley or

Vinho Verdes from Portugal. But what if wine drinkers might want to have a glass of the former with oysters or something refreshingly low in alcohol like the latter?

When winter arrives, according to all seasonal wine pushers, you'd better be drinking a seasonal red—which is to say a big wine with a lot of structure and tannin and probably alcohol too—like a Zinfandel or a Cabernet or a Syrah. Of course that's based on the assumption that you're eating pasta Bolognese or some really rich dish. Here again I'd like to make a plea for diversity of taste: there are plenty of people who prefer salad to stew, even in the darkest and coldest months of the year.

Maybe it all comes down to a matter of buying and selling—of wine merchants who need to offer customers some context for the sale and customers who need some reason to favor one wine over another. And if it's not going to be based on a number (aka a wine critic's score), I guess it might as well be in accordance with Mother Nature. But then I'm not sure she's any more of a reliable source.

Copying the Code

THE FRENCH HAVE DONE SO MUCH FOR THE WORLD. Ask any Frenchman and he will doubtless confirm that this is true. French food alone could—and has—credited a very large global debt, as have the French fashion and the French phrasing. Drop a French bon mot or two and you'll seem quite dashing (as long as you pronounce it properly, of course). But it's the French wine laws that have left us fully indebted to our Gallic confrères.

The French system of *Appellation d'Origine Contrôlée* is one of the most-copied laws in the world; it's been applied everywhere, and not just to wine but also to spirits and food. There is an *Appellation d'Origine Contrôlée* cheese and meat and Cognac. Everyone seems to have his or her version of this system—which seems as if it's been around forever but was actually created almost a hundred years ago (although it has been refined and adapted ever since).

The French *d'origine contrôlée* was created as a means of ensuring that certain wines were actually produced in particular places with particular grapes. Wines labeled "Bordeaux" had to be made in the region and only from certain permitted grapes. For example, Cabernet Sauvignon and Merlot were sanctioned in Bordeaux, but Pinot Noir was not. It had to do with history and tradition, and it was a practical consideration, too: in a cold, rainy climate like Bordeaux, Pinot Noir could rot.

The laws were created, in part, to combat serious fraud; a hundred years ago, grapes from Algeria might easily show up under the label of "Châteauneuf-du-Pape." But the French wine laws go well beyond regions and grapes and also cover how large the yields can be and when the harvest must take place. This is all overseen by the government—the muscle behind the AOC.

The Germans and Italians have created their own forms of wine governance, though perhaps none are as strong and as clear as the French. The American system follows the French in a more freewheeling style, especially in some of the newer wine regions. For example, there are no specifically permitted grape varieties on the North Fork of Long Island, although it is an official wine appellation.

Things are a bit more restrictive in the more famous places in this country—the Napa Valley is perhaps the best example of how much Americans have taken the protectionist French wine laws to heart. About ten years ago, the Napa powers that be took aim at various attempts to co-opt its name and proposed a Napa Valley name law. This law morphed into a joint declaration as other famous winemaking regions like Paso Robles, Chablis, and Chianti Classico later signed onto the declaration as well. (Those last two have had their names abused by American makers of cheap wines for a lot longer than Napa had its name bandied about.)

Napa winemakers were able to wrest a few legal concessions in China, a country more famous for the talent of its counterfeiters than its winemakers. Apparently the "Napa" name was showing up on quite a few labels of wines made in China (or heaven knows where). The Napa Valley vintners were able to convince the Chinese government to grant Napa Valley official recognition and protection of its name.

I'm not sure how this will be enforced from thousands of miles away, but if such a law can work in a country like China, then it's a remarkable victory and one that clearly must be credited to those who created it: the French.

Four Letter Freedom

ALTHOUGH A GOOD WINE LIST IS EXCITING and a good somme-lier can be inspiring, nothing makes me happier than dining in a restaurant that allows diners to BYOB. These four letters—which stand for "bring your own bottle"—describe one of the great privileges of dining for most oenophiles.

Of course, certain restaurants—and certain cities—are more BYOB-friendly than others. Some places don't permit the practice at all. For example, I've never been able to bring a bottle to a restaurant in Dallas, while San Francisco is an incredibly BYOB-happy town. In New York, it depends on the restaurant and the person—and sometimes, how much you're willing to pay. Some restaurants charge a "corkage fee" of between fifty and one hundred dollars for each bottle you bring along. This would make me think twice about bringing a bottle at all.

I happen to live in the exceptionally BYOB-friendly state of New Jersey. Here restaurants are much more likely to be BYOB than not. That's not because the state legislators are all fervent wine lovers with extensive private cellars but because New Jersey has some of the most antiquated liquor laws in the country. There is actually a cap on the number of liquor licenses in any town in New Jersey, and the number is established by the population of that particular town. That means if you want to open a restaurant and there aren't any liquor licenses available, you're stuck with the status of BYOB.

For me, this is almost sufficient compensation for the fact that New Jersey has some of the highest property taxes in the country, not to mention some of the worst traffic jams and the worst roads. In fact, I can't see any great benefit to living in the state of New Jersey without the ongoing privi-lege of BYOB.

The idea that the wine choice is entirely yours—matching your particular mood and oenological predilections—is nearly as compelling as the fact that you are saving lots of money. The mark-up on a bottle of wine can be as much as three hundred or four hundred percent in a restaurant in New York—and sometimes even more.

But because it's, above all, a privilege, I have my own BYOB rules. The first has to do with tipping. I always tip as if there were a thirty- to forty-dollar bottle of wine on my check. The tip is never less than twenty-five percent, sometimes as much as thirty percent for particularly good service. (My husband, a New Jersey native, had never thought of doing this before we met; now he is a thirty-percenter as well.)

Secondly, if the list is interesting and there are some good selections that are well priced, I'll buy a wine too. This isn't applicable if there are only two people dining but with a group of four or more. It shows respect for the restaurant and the sommelier (if there is one). And if there is a sommelier, I will always offer him or her a taste of my wine. Or, in the case of my favorite BYOB restaurant, Divina, in Caldwell, New Jersey, I'll offer a taste to the chef.

Divina's chef and owner Mario Carlino knows a great deal about wine—especially Italian wine—and I try to bring wine that shows my respect for his palate as well as his food. He likes Barolo and fine Chianti and white wines from Campania—although he's a native of Calabria. He's quite discriminating in his tastes. In fact, there is nothing quite so crushing as when Chef Carlino approaches our table, sees what we're drinking, and passes us by without asking for a taste.

On occasion, he will tell us what someone else is drinking, sometimes bringing us a glass. We'll return the favor, and suddenly there will be a great flurry of glasses going back and forth across the room. I've almost never witnessed this sort of spontaneous sharing in restaurants where people are buying wines from a list. Perhaps that's the best part about BYOB. It's not just about drinking wine but making new friends.

Learning about wine is a lot like learning a language. You can read books and take classes, but you can't stop there. You need a context for what you've learned and you must practice it every day. Fortunately, in the case of wine, that means drinking.

Need to Know

The Magic Number

ALTHOUGH EVERY WINE DRINKER I KNOW agrees on this number, very few can explain how 55 degrees Fahrenheit came to represent the ideal wine storage temperature. But 55 is. In fact, the most-cited number by collectors and wine storage companies—it's even the name of some wine bars and stores.

I've read that the number comes from the fact that 55 is the temperature of a European cellar—as if there were such a thing as one collective cellar throughout. That's fifty countries' worth of 55-degree cellars.

This isn't a number that most people have to worry about, of course, since few wines in the world actually benefit from extended aging (more than a year or two) and few people actually have temperature-controlled storage. Far more wine drinkers, I suspect, have wine storage that is actually a part of a pantry or the back of a shelf.

And then there is the fact that there isn't such thing as a purely perfect temperature any more than there is one that is completely consistent. Temperature fluctuates, even in a supposedly temperature-controlled environment like a wine cabinet. (Open the door a few times and you'll see what I mean; the temperature will shift a few degrees.)

And it's temperature stability—over the long term—that's key. A few degrees up or down the temperature scale isn't a huge deal—it's the really big swings that will do in the wine. And yet some of the same people who believe there is such a thing as uniformity of European cellars also maintain that every degree over 55 degrees ages a wine by a full year and once you get over 70 degrees, it's said to be even faster, each degree equalling something closer to a decade.

I've never tested this math—and I'm not even sure how I would even if I had the desire or more importantly the time, but I do know that the lower the temperature the slower the aging effect on the wine. (Sadly this does not seem to apply to people. No matter how cold your basement might be, you'll still be aging just as fast.)

A wine that is stored at 50 degrees or even 45 degrees will age much more slowly than a wine stored at 55. So if you really want your wine to mature long after you do, set your thermometer down a few degrees more. But don't set it down too far. You don't want the wine to freeze—or to live on without you.

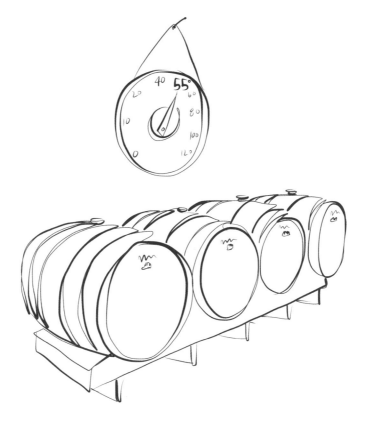

A G'day to Grow Grapes

FEW WINEMAKING COUNTRIES have swung from boom to bust more often and more widely than Australia. Actually there has been a bit less boom and more bust in Australia over the past decade or so. There was the matter of flooding the market with excess production, and then there was the matter of drought. The biggest one was called the Millennium Drought and lasted an incredible fourteen years—from 1995 to 2009.

Then there was the matter of the inflated Australian dollar, which discouraged Australian producers from shipping their non-price-competitive wines to markets overseas. This caused some Aussie labels to virtually disappear. And then there was the matter of changing tastes: wine drinkers turned away from high-octane Shiraz, the specialty of Australia, to lower-alcohol options from other places in the world.

And then of course there was the matter of those animal brands. Australian companies of the large corporate kind flooded the market with wines whose labels bore pictures of penguins, frogs, and kangaroos, making Australia seem less like a serious winemaking country than a petting zoo. Sophisticated oenophiles looked elsewhere for more subtle, more polished, less silly-looking wines.

And yet Australian wine produces a great many subtle and serious wines too. They're what I call the Alternate Australians—the wines that don't fit the clichés of the cheap and cheerful Australian Shiraz. They're from small, lesser-known regions like Tasmania and the Yarra and Clare Valleys.

Tasmania is perhaps the most interesting of the three wine regions—it's certainly the most unique. Located just off the country's southern coast, Tasmania's cool climate is just right for ripening grapes like Chardonnay and Pinot Noir and for making sparkling wine from those same grapes too. One of the most interesting sparkling wines in Australia—and perhaps even the New World—is Jansz, whose producers describe their winemaking method not as *méthode Champenoise* as most quality producers do but, in cheeky Aussie fashion, *méthode Tasmanoise*.

The Yarra Valley, east of Melbourne, is another cool-climate region where some very good wines are produced and a great deal of wine tourism takes place. The valley is a particularly notable source of wines made from Pinot Noir and Chardonnay, which are in turn also utilized in making some very good sparkling wine. (Domaine Chandon, the Oz outpost of Moët & Chandon, is located here.) Another top producer, Coldstream Hills, makes terrific Pinot Noir. It's one of the best-known wineries in the Yarra Valley and it was founded by James Halliday, Australia's most famous wine writer.

The Clare Valley, north of Adelaide, is one of my favorite Australian regions; it's not only home to some terrific Riesling but also the source of some very good Shiraz. Although it gets fairly hot during the day, the Clare Valley gets quite cool at night. It's a perfect condition for growing good Riesling (and a more refined sort of Shiraz). A Clare Valley Riesling is quite dry and often intensely aromatic—it's usually bigger and riper than a Riesling from the Mosel in Germany and not as high in acidity as one from New Zealand or the Finger Lakes of New York. They're lively and vivacious, and the best wines (from producers like Jim Barry and Jeffrey Grosset) can last a very long time.

These Alternate Australians may not keep another wine crisis from unfolding, but they might give wine drinkers a different perspective on the country—and a good reason to give the wines of Oz another try.

Your Merchant the Mensch

EVERYONE KNOWS THE IMPORTANCE of knowing a skilled dentist, a sympathetic hairdresser, or an agile masseuse, but what about a reliable wine merchant with a palate and a pricing strategy you trust?

Most Americans are said to do most of their wine shopping at grocery stores, but they'd be better off patronizing an independent wine retailer who doesn't just sell bottles but also dispenses (good) advice. A retailer worth his or her salt (or Chardonnay) can talk about vintages, regions, and up-and-coming producers and counsel his or her customers about what is—and is not—a good deal.

That's the ideal scenario, to be sure, and there are some retailers who offer more sound—or more honest—judgments about wine than others. And there are retailers who rely too much on the scores awarded by critics or whose taste might not necessarily coincide with your own. How do you tell who's right for you? There are a number of wine merchants whose advice, taste, and insight I rely upon, and here are a few reasons why I will shop at their stores over and over again.

Integrity

This is the most important quality that a good wine retailer can possess. It can be anything from selling wines that they actually have in stock (there's a lot of bait and switch in the wine world) to taking back bottles that are flawed. It's a merchant who sells wines that he or she believes in and not because of a supplier discount.

Reliability

This seems like a pretty obvious requirement in a retailer (or for that matter, a dentist or hairdresser), but a retailer who sells wines that you fall in love with over and over again (and I'm not talking about the same wine) is someone who has reliable taste. Or at least a palate that aligns nicely with yours.

Resourcefulness

Some wine merchants are better at finding wines than others. If I'm looking for a particular wine, there are certain merchants who will do anything to find that bottle for me—and they will price it fairly when they do. Some wine merchants have better relationships with key importers and wholesalers who are happy to do them a few favors. These wine merchants are definitely worth knowing.

Balanced adventurousness

I like a retailer who mixes the tried-and-true with the unknown. I don't want every bottle to be from an obscure part of the world. I find that kind of preciousness as annoying as the laziness of a retailer who stocks wines according to their Parker scores.

Reasonable pricing

This last item needs no further explanation. There are wine shops with good selections that I no longer patronize because their markups are simply too large. When every wine in their store is five or ten dollars more than it is in another shop farther away, I'll travel the distance (or better yet, have it delivered) rather than patronize a wine merchant who takes my money and who also clearly believes—or counts on the fact—that I'm uninformed. (That's the beauty of the Internet and particularly wine-searcher.com. No store can escape from price comparison today.)

Bordeaux for Beginners

WHEN WOULD-BE OENOPHILES are learning about wine, one of the first places they tend to explore is Bordeaux. There are several possible reasons why this is the case, but my own theory is that it's because Bordeaux is the most hierarchical wine region in the world.

Novice wine drinkers appreciate hierarchy and rankings that seem to give some sort of guidance as to a wine's (purported) quality, and worth. The Bordeaux quite helpfully provide this, ranking its châteaux numerically from one to five. (First to fifth "growths"—but more on that later.) In other wine regions like Burgundy and Alsace or the Rheingau in Germany, it's the vineyards that are rated with words like *grand* and *premier cru*. They are not only more numerous but considerably messier, as there are hundreds of vineyards and many times they're cut up into very small pieces. One vineyard might have dozens of owners who may or may not share the same standards.

The Bordeaux system, officially known as the Classification of 1855, started as a one-off for a big fair in Paris. Not just any fair but a kind of world's fair at the behest of Napoleon III himself. Bordeaux wine merchants got together to create an official ranking of their best-selling (and presumably highest quality) châteaux. They called each level a "growth," aka "cru" in French, and ranked them from first to fifth. The ranking was based on price, though presumably quality as well: the most expensive—and one would hope the best—wines were the first growths and the least impressive and the cheapest were the fifth.

Of course, there are plenty of Bordeaux wines that were left unrated—all of the dry white wines and all the wines on the Right Bank of Bordeaux. There were no sweet wines rated either, save for Château d'Yquem, which was rated all on its own. (The 1855 Sauternes-Barsac Classification was a separate ranking for sweet wines.) Clearly there were a lot of unspectacular wines being made back in the time of the classification—or perhaps it was lots of Bordeaux producers who lacked the requisite clout.

The list wasn't inclusive, but it wasn't actually meant to be—after all, there were only fifty-eight châteaux on the list and there were (and are) hundreds and hundreds of châteaux in Bordeaux. It was a reflection of the wines that the merchants thought mattered and were worth more money than most.

Remarkably, the original ranking remains almost unaltered, with one notable exception: a single château that ascended from second to first. Thanks to Baron Philippe de Rothschild's relentless lobbying efforts, Château Mouton Rothschild was elevated to first growth status in 1973. No one else since has had the time, money, or perhaps the stubbornness of will to effect any further changes. (Perhaps the powers that be in Bordeaux vowed not to let it happen again on their watch?)

Whether the Bordeaux classification is still accurate today is a question with a very long and highly political answer. Some wine professionals—and châteaux owners—think that certain châteaux should be elevated. And some think that other châteaux should be demoted. So far nothing has changed—at least in terms of the ranking. But as more and more of the great Bordeaux châteaux change hands from winemaking families to corporations, perhaps future wine drinkers will think about Bordeaux châteaux not in terms of a hierarchy but as name brands.

From Grape to Glass

HOW MUCH—OR HOW LITTLE—do you need or want to know about how wine is made? Unless you're planning a winemaking career, learning how the wine got into the bottle is likely to be enough.

The basics of winemaking are pretty straightforward and involve a series of steps. The first step is to take the freshly harvested grapes and crush them. This releases the sugars for fermentation, which is the process of transforming sugar into alcohol. (The higher the sugar, the higher the potential alcohol of the wine.)

The fermentation process is aided by the presence of yeast, either natural or cultivated. (There are all types of cultivated yeasts, each one tailored for a specific purpose or even a specific wine.) The yeasts must be just warm enough to keep working; if the temperature is too low or too high, fermentation will stop. This is called a "stuck" fermentation, and unless the winemaker has stopped it deliberately (more on that later), it's a big problem. The fermentation has to be started again—especially if the winemaker wants the wine to be dry. (Remember, there is still sugar that's yet to be converted to alcohol.)

Some wines that are deliberately stopped mid-stride are sweet, fortified wines such as Port. This is called an "arrested" fermentation (the fermentation word choices can be rather dramatic). There are different fermentation techniques—and times—for red, white, and sparkling wine. Red wine, for example, is often fermented at a higher temperature than white wine. But too fast or too hot a fermentation could result in a wine that tastes "cooked"; its aromas and flavors could be pretty bad.

There are also practical considerations when it comes to fermentation time: if a winemaker needs his fermentation tanks for a new batch of wine, he might speed a fermentation along. The newly fermented wine is left alone for a few days to let all the sedimentary bits of the wine settle to the bottom, after which it is racked, which involves pumping the wine away from the sediment. Then it might be refined or clarified—a step some winemakers eschew, thinking it strips away character too. Their wines are often a bit cloudy as a result.

A second fermentation, called malolactic fermentation, often takes place to soften the wine. This is done to most red wines and many white wines, save for those like Riesling and Sauvignon Blanc that are meant to be rather high acidity. After this the wine (especially red) may be racked into barrels. Whites may be transferred to barrels or stainless-steel tanks.

At this point the winemakers are looking to minimize the wine's exposure to oxygen, so they might add a bit of sulfur dioxide, which acts as a preservative. (Some winemakers add none or very little as a matter of a "naturalist" philosophy—a very long story—and this can make their wines unstable, particularly in terms of storage and shipping.)

Bottling is the last step and it takes place anytime from a few months (for white wines and Rosés meant to be consumed fresh and young) to years—even decades—later, depending on the wine and the winemakers' philosophy.

Those are the bare bones of the basic winemaking process. There are lots more specifics, of course, and greater details, much of which is shared on winery websites. That's because winemakers—and by extension winery marketing teams—love to talk about the way their particular wine is made. It's biology, it's chemistry, and it's art.

All Chalked Up

IMITATION IS SAID TO BE THE SINCEREST FORM OF FLATTERY. In the case of wine, it may also be one way of telling if it is truly great. Consider, for example, Chablis. There are few wines that have been more often imitated over the years. There has been pink Chablis, Mountain Chablis, and, of course, "California" Chablis courtesy of the Gallo company.

Chablis stood for a sort of dry, palatable white wine whose greatest hallmark was the fact it was cheap. And Chablis was in illustrious company: there were also ersatz red Burgundies, Port, and even Sauternes—except that with fake Sauterne, unlike the real dessert wine from France, there was no "s" at the end.

Of course, there is only one real Chablis, one wine by that name that is truly great (not to mention legitimate). It's made from the Chardonnay grape and grown in the Chablis region of France just south of Paris. (Chablis is one of the five subregions of Burgundy, although on a map it looks like it should be part of Champagne.)

Chablis and Champagne have a lot in common—even their soil is similar, a chalky white limestone soil that's rather dramatically beautiful, even more so when it shows up on the other side of the channel as the White Cliffs of Dover.

The soil of Chablis is actually thousands of years old and is full of fossils and minerals and even oyster shells dating back thousands of years to when Chablis was actually underwater. This may be why people sometimes compare the taste of a great Chablis to oyster shells (though admittedly it can sound a tad pretentious).

Chablis has a truly distinctive flavor profile; it's flinty, minerally, and very dry. It also has fairly high acidity of a very particular sort. It's very bright and clean—almost shimmering in the glass. In fact, you might hear someone say of a white wine possessed of particular clarity: "It's like a Chablis."

There are several types of Chablis. Just as in the Côte d'Or (the other great Burgundy subregion), there is a quality hierarchy, starting with Petit Chablis—wines made from grapes grown on the tops of the hills, the least desirable soils. Chablis may be the only great wine region with a "Petite" version of the regular stuff.

Next are the basic wines made from grapes grown anywhere in the region that are called simply "Chablis." All the great producers make these basic versions as well as the fancier premier and grand crus, and their basic wines can be terrific deals. The "basic" Chablis are best consumed within a couple of years of the vintage, although they can sometimes last surprisingly long. I once had a twelve-year-old Chablis at a restaurant in New York that was quite good, and an incredible bargain for the price—less than thirty dollars on the wine list.

Premier cru Chablis is a bit higher up the ladder in terms of quality. These are wines made from vineyards designated premier cru for their purported capacity to produce wines of greater intensity and depth. And finally, there are seven grand cru vineyards whose wines are considered the very best. These are wines that can age beautifully and become richer in flavor and texture and deeper in color. A well-structured grand cru Chablis can easily develop in complexity and interest for ten years or more depending on vintage and producer. And unlike grand cru Burgundies of the Côte-d'Or, grand cru Chablis is actually almost ridiculously affordable. It's at least one digit and often two digits cheaper than its Côte-d'Or counterpart: a grand cru Chablis can cost as little as seventy-five dollars, while a white Burgundy from a grand cru vineyard in the Côte-d'Or like Montrachet could easily cost ten times as much. In other words, Chablis is a wine that collectors covet but one that mere mortals—and wine writers—can actually collect.

A few of my favorite Chablis producers include Dauvissat, Raveneau, Christian Moreau, and William Fèvre; with the exception of Raveneau, who has a cultlike following (unusual in Chablis), their wines are all fairly easy to find. And that's another big selling point for Chablis.

Chablis is also a wine that sommeliers adore because it pairs well with food, thanks to its bright acidity, but also because it's unlikely to have been aged in oak. Oak is a tough match with food; it can flatten rather than enhance flavor.

And finally, Chablis is simply a joy to pronounce. Its name glides alone in a sibilant fashion that's more like a caress than a word—just as the wine itself does in the glass.

Cook's Choice

THERE'S ONE WINE QUESTION that I'm asked on occasion but that still stumps me over and over again: What's a good cooking wine? It's not because I don't cook with wine, because I do—and pretty often. But if someone asks me specifically for a wine to cook with, I always answer: It depends.

It depends, first of all, on the kind of wine that the recipe calls for; most recipes give general directions about the type of wine required (e.g., a dry white or dry red), although some recipes are more specific, citing the need for a Riesling or a Pinot Noir or even a specific brand—though this may have more to do with magazine advertisers than it does with the actual recipe.

It also depends on what you want to drink, since most people I know intermingle the two: the drinking wine becomes the cooking wine and the cooking wine becomes the drinking wine (which can be a bit dangerous when knives are in use).

I don't tend to drink and cook or, for that matter, drink what I cook with. Instead, I treat the two as separate wines, especially if it's a wine whose flavor might show up in the dish. It also depends on whether the wine will be an important ingredient or just a last-minute splash of liquid to deglaze the pan. If it's a key ingredient in the dish, the wine quality might not be something to overlook.

Some people choose the wine depending on what they plan to cook. My friend Gabrielle isn't usually discerning about the wine that she uses in her cooking ("anything that's open" is her sole qualification) unless the dish is chicken or a soup, which she thinks will transmit more of the flavors of the wine. In this case she will cook with a wine that's fruity and "not too overpowering," like a Riesling, she said.

My friend Allison favors fruity wines too; she believes that they add a dimension to the dish that a higher-acid, more minerally wine does not, despite the fact that she doesn't like fruity wine. (That's why she buys the cheapest fruity wine possible.)

The one cooking wine that I won't touch is the type that is actually labeled "cooking wine" and is sold in grocery stores (but not in the wine section). More often than not it contains additives such as salt and potassium sorbate and potassium metabisulfite. Are those really ingredients that you think will enhance the food?

On the other hand, I have to admit I was curious about a cooking wine that I found online. The Pompeian "Burgundy" cooking wine contains the usual salt and preservatives, but it's also a cooking wine that is labeled "Burgundy wine from Spain." The accompanying sales pitch promises a "robust, premium, Spanish Burgundy wine." That's something I want to try: France and Spain in a single bottle. That's a lot of geography for a two-dollar wine.

The Country of Cheap

THERE ARE WORSE CHARACTERIZATIONS OF A WINE than "cheap and cheerful" (although the producers of such wines might argue otherwise). But the words *cheap* and *cheerful* show up over and over again whenever people describe the wines from Chile.

Chile has been producing wine for hundreds of years, but it wasn't until the 1990s that their wines made a global mark. Fortunately or unfortunately, that happened to be in the sub-ten-dollar category, a place from which they've never fully escaped even though the overall quality of Chilean wines has risen considerably.

Chilean Merlots and Sauvignon Blancs soon found a niche in American wine shops—or, more often, grocery stores. They were sought after so long as they didn't cost very much. And although there are serious Chilean wines priced far above the ten-dollar mark, the world at large hasn't really caught on to this fact since ten-dollar Chilean wines are still very good.

One of the reasons that Chile is so little understood or appreciated may have to do with geography. The most important winemaking regions in Chile (e.g., Casablanca, Maipo, Colchagua, and Maule) are quite obscure for most American wine drinkers, who still seem to buy Chilean wines not by the place of origin but the price.

But what if these wine drinkers looked a bit closer at Chilean terroir? Odds are, they'd find regions as distinct from one another as, say, Burgundy from Bordeaux. Take, for example, Casablanca (a great name for a wine region as well as a movie). It's a cool, fog-shrouded region just a few miles from the ocean where some of the country's best white wines are produced, notably Sauvignon Blanc and Chardonnay.

Casablanca is a pretty new discovery for Chilean vintners, having only been planted in the 1980s. And there are two even cooler, even younger, and some think potentially even better winemaking regions nearby as well: San Antonio and Leyda. (The latter is a source of some truly terrific Sauvignon Blanc.) But they're not as famous, perhaps because they don't have a cinematic-sounding hook.

The Maipo Valley is Chile's oldest and most significant wine region, with several wineries dating back some 150 years. Some of the most famous wineries—Santa Rita and Concha y Toro—are based there. Maipo is mostly important for structured and serious Bordeaux-style reds, including Concha y Toro's Don Melchor, the first famous wine from Chile. (And one that is still remarkably cheap; a bottle can cost as little as fifty dollars, making it perhaps the most affordable flagship wine of any country in the world.)

The other two important regions, Maule and Colchagua, are harder to pronounce and have too many vowels. And yet Colchagua is likened to Napa by Chileans, as it's home to their most important red wine producers. Cabernet, Merlot, and Carménère are the key grapes in both regions, though Syrah and Malbec do well in Colchagua, and the Casa Lapostolle Winery is probably Colchagua's biggest name.

The Maule Valley is far from Santiago and perhaps for that reason the least known and the most often overlooked. It was also home to a lot of cheap stuff that wasn't necessarily cheerful. But the quality has been improving, and Maule produces a wide range of mostly red wines—Cabernet, Carignan, Malbec, and Merlot—although there is also Chardonnay and Sauvignon Blanc. (There's even some Pinot Noir.)

There are many more adjectives that could be employed to describe Chilean wines beyond *cheerful* and *cheap*—like *ambitious* and *sound*. Maybe Chilean wines will never achieve a level of prestige that other wine countries possess (there are too many of its wines in the grocery stores), but there are Chilean wines of remarkable character and historical significance and—yes—value, too.

From Ubiquity to Inequity

SOME WINES ARE FAMOUS, SOME MUCH BELOVED, while others are simply . . . ubiquitous. Such was the case with Chianti—at least for a while.

A fixture on every American wine list, whether the restaurant was Italian or not, Chianti was as easy to drink as it was to pronounce. It wasn't complex or challenging or even good, but it came in a cute straw-covered bottle (called a *fiasco*) that when emptied made an especially charming candle holder.

But things have changed greatly over the years. Chianti became serious, even expensive, and no longer ubiquitous. This was good for the image of Chianti and the best producers of it, even if that meant the lesser producers got left behind.

Chianti producers began experimenting with nontraditional grapes like Cabernet and Merlot to blend with Sangiovese, the indigenous grape of Tuscany. This was a definite step up from the grapes they were using before, like Trebbiano, a bland, characterless white grape. The wines were generally much better, but the traditionalist winemakers of Chianti were appalled. Cabernet and Merlot were not Tuscan. Even an all-Sangiovese wine was deemed heretical—even if it was often pretty good. To the hidebound old-school producers, what was traditional was often more important than what was good.

The experimenters had to settle for labeling their wines "vino da tavola," which basically meant "table wine." But once they started getting so much attention—and commanding so much more money than "real" Chianti—the Italian government eventually changed its tune. A new appellation label, "IGT" *indicazione geografica tipica* was introduced, giving a certain amount of freedom to winemakers.

They were forced to recognize that the maverick producers' wines were much better than their more traditional counterparts, and so little by little they changed the laws. First they allowed all-Sangiovese wines to be labeled as Chianti, and later they even allowed Chiantis with a bit of Cabernet and Merlot.

Today's Chiantis may not be recognizable from those wines of the old days—they're not as easy to find and they're definitely not as cheap as they were—but they aren't wines that anyone would think to call a "fiasco," let alone use as a candlestick.

Just Desserts

IF AMERICANS CARED HALF AS MUCH about dessert wines as they do desserts, the fortunes of Port producers, Sherry makers, and all wine-makers in obscure places like Rivesaltes and Banyuls would be all but assured. Alas, we aren't really a country of après-dinner drinkers. Our dinner chaser of choice is more often . . . ice cream.

Dessert wine is seen as alternately unsophisticated ("great wines, after all, are dry and preferably red") or self-indulgent ("do you really need all that sugar coupled with alcohol as well?"). And yet dessert wines are actually some of the most complex, most sophisticated, and most intriguing wines in the world. Their range can be enormous, from the barely sweet (an Italian Moscato or a German Spätlese) to the treacly (an Australian Muscat—rightfully nicknamed by Australians as "sticky").

While the dessert wine category is far too large to cover in such a short space (consider the correlative absurdity of an essay on "dry" wines), there are three sweet wines that I truly love and that I think wine drinkers should know (more) about.

Moscato d'Asti is my favorite dessert wine on the light and fizzy side. It's not the Moscato that rap stars sing about, but the one that is produced in the Asti district of the Piedmont region of Italy. It's delicate and bright, refreshing and low alcohol. The perfect accompaniment is a simple piece of fruit—perhaps a ripe pear—making it almost a diet drink. One of my favorites is made by Ceretto, who also happens to make great reds in Piedmont too.

My second favorite is a dessert wine that experienced a brief flare of popularity a couple of decades ago and then pretty much disappeared. Muscat de Beaumes-de-Venise, one of the hundreds of dessert wines made all over the world from the ever-so-useful Muscat grape. (Moscato and Muscat, by the way, are the same grape, just very different styles of wine).

There is also Muscat Blanc à Petit Grains Blanc, a sweet wine from the Rhône Valley. It has a history of greatness (Pliny the Elder was apparently a fan) and is relatively low alcohol (15 percent). There are also non-sweet Beaumes (as it's sometimes called), both red and white, but the dessert version is a delicate wine whose beguiling aromas are a large part of its appeal (think bergamot tea and orange peel). It's not too light or too heavy; it's the perfect wine to serve with a tart (of any sort). My favorite producer is Domaine de Durban.

Vintage Port is my favorite of all the big, rich dessert wines, the polar opposite of Moscato in terms of weight and alcohol (about 16 percent versus about 10 percent). It's not only the greatest wine of Portugal but one of the great wonders of the world. There are actually many Port incarnations (tawny, ruby, late-bottled vintage, single quinta vintage, and of course vintage), but vintage Port is the grail.

Vintage Port represents a small fraction of Port production (no more than 2 percent of all Ports are vintage), but it's definitely the most prestigious wine of the region. Produced from the very best grapes in only the very best years (a great vintage is universally "declared" by Port producers—roughly three are declared per decade), vintage Port is aged a few years in wood, then bottled. A great vintage Port from a great producer (Taylor-Fladgate, Graham's, Dow's) from a truly stellar vintage can takes years, if not decades to mature. It's a wine of another era, an intellectual as well as gustatory treat.

Americans may be drinking more "dessert" wines than they realize. After all, the country's wine laws label any wine over 14 percent alcohol as a "dessert wine," which could include many Napa Valley Cabernets and Sonoma Zinfandels and perhaps even a few Chardonnays. (Wines can be fermented dry at much higher levels of alcohol than they were back when this law was passed.) Maybe wine drinkers who are in fear of dessert wines should consider having a glass of a low-alcohol Moscato—and a little less Cab.

Grooving on Grüner

EVERY ONCE IN A WHILE, a grape seizes the collective imagination of wine drinkers everywhere in the world (or at least the United States) and it never abates. Pinot Noir is perhaps the leading example of this fact. There's no end in sight for lovers—and producers—of Pinot Noir. Ditto Chardonnay, though it's less regularly lauded and its death was predicted decades ago by non-Chardonnay fans who adopted a hostile elementary acronym (ABC—Anything but Chardonnay) to prove their point.

Grüner Veltliner may be the closest grape to Pinot Noir in terms of its ongoing popularity and respect. Some fifteen or so years after its debut in this country, Grüner Veltliner is still going strong.

Sommeliers were the first, most passionate Grüner groupies—mostly because Grüner is such a great match with food. It's dry but not too dry, aromatic but not too aromatic—more white pepper and spice than lavender and roses. It's not too lean and not too rich, and its acidity just kind of tingles in your mouth.

Grüner Veltliner is the star grape of Austria; although some Austrian winemakers might tell you that they personally favor Austrian Riesling, Grüner is their workhorse grape. Grüner Veltliner is grown in other countries as well, especially in the Alto Adige region of northern Italy (which belonged to Austria before World War I). Grüner Veltliner has even been planted in California, Washington State, and New York in recent years.

Grüner Veltliner also has the advantage of a name that's fun to pronounce, although some people put the emphasis on the wrong syllable. Say "Grooner Velt-LEENER," not "GrOONer Veltliner." (I was taught the correct pronunciation by my former neighbor, an Austrian-born

"Grooner Velt – **LEENER**"

"GrOO - VEE"

Freudian analyst.) Some have made Grüner's name even hipper, turning it into Groo-Vee. And Grüner Veltliner can be found at a reasonable price: it's easy to find a good wine for less than fifteen bucks, often in a liter-sized bottle.

But there is also serious Grüner Veltliner too—and this is essential to any popular wine. There must be elevated examples as well. There are single-vineyard, small-production Grüners that can cost hundreds of dollars and are much sought after. Most of these wines come from the picturesque Wachau region of Austria, which even has its own ranking system for Grüner Veltliner and Riesling.

The Wachau system divides the wines into three types: the lightest wines are called Steinfeders; they are simple wines meant to be drunk in their youth. The second category of wines are a bit more sturdy and higher in alcohol—they're called Federspiel. The third category is composed of wines called Smaragd, which are rich and quite powerful and also dry. These are the longest-lived Grüner Veltliners in the Wachau. (The three designations actually apply to Rieslings, too.) These categories aren't in use anywhere else in Austria, and it's unlikely that anyone who isn't a sommelier or Grüner Veltliner–obsessed drinker knows what they mean, let alone how they're (correctly) pronounced.

Will Grüner Veltliner remain as beloved as Pinot Noir or even Chardonnay? The wine-drinking public can be fickle, after all (producers of Syrah know this), and sommeliers change their minds as often as they do their wine lists. But with its long list of virtues, I'm betting Grüner Veltliner will be popular with American wine drinkers for a long time—perhaps even long enough to become officially Groo-Vee.

The Explorers' Club

FAMOUS WINE BRANDS ARE EASY TO FIND: from Yellow Tail to Dom Pérignon, their names are emblazoned on labels for all to see. But there are also some wine importers whose choices are so reliably good that they have become wine brands themselves. Importers like Kermit Lynch, Neal Rosenthal, and Terry Theise are so skilled at choosing wines that wine drinkers speak of "a Kermit Lynch wine" much as they would any other brand name.

These three men are just a few of the dozen or so American wine importers whose names are considered guarantees that a wine will be good—and not only good but one that will carry a "true sense of place."

Importers like Mr. Lynch and Mr. Rosenthal were not the first American importers of note—there were men of an earlier generation, such as American wine importer Alexis Lichine (and, yes, they were always men in those days), whose names also showed up on the back labels of wine bottles (and sometimes the strip above the front label as well).

But Mssrs. Lynch, Rosenthal, et al. were at the vanguard of modern winemaking in the world some twenty or thirty years ago. They started in countries like France, Italy and Spain, and Germany and discovered some of the best small producers in places and regions that many wine drinkers in this country had never heard of before, such as Touraine in the Loire Valley, Roussillon in southern France, the Marches region of Italy, and Baden or Nahe in Germany.

These importers inspired a generation of men and women (though not nearly as many women) determined to do the same. They followed their mentors into some of those very same countries—and went beyond them too, exploring countries like Slovenia, New Zealand, and Australia. Some of these importers have also acquired recognizable names, but many more do not—at least not yet.

I asked Mr. Theise what he thought about his evolution from wine importer to brand; his reply was modest but direct. The greatest benefit was to the producers whose wines he represented, said Mr. Theise. The fact that the winemakers' work was recognized and that they could sell their wines for a good price was what he regarded as a great part of his success. (Mr. Theise imports high-quality Austrian and German wines as well as small-grower Champagnes—a category he pretty much created in this country.)

When Mr. Theise launched his company a few decades ago, very few people in the United States were drinking Austrian wines or knew anything about Champagnes that weren't made by big names like Perrier-Jouët and Moët & Chandon. But Mr. Theise, in a move of marketing brilliance, called his Champagne growers "farmers" to distinguish them from the big commercial houses, and he called their wines "farmer fizz." It immediately caught on. What oenophile wouldn't want his or her fizz to come from a farmer?

As for that part about being a brand, it was a responsibility as well as a privilege, according to Mr. Theise. It helped to sell the wines, of course, but he also felt a great deal of pressure to make sure his customers were "almost never disappointed—and that's harder than it sounds."

Actually, that sounded pretty hard to me. Almost never disappointing someone, especially with a bottle of wine, is quite a feat. But Mr. Theise and his peers seem to have mastered this. Their wines are just that reliable. And that's how they transformed themselves from "mere" salesmen of wines to their own brands.

New York
State of Mind

WHAT DID IT TAKE TO TURN A STATE FAMOUS FOR PIZZA and politics and a certain state of mind (according to Billy Joel) into a place that's a bit famous for wine? The answer: about fifty years. That's how long it took for New York to be recognized as a source of good wine.

There are several places in New York where good wine is made—the first and probably the most famous is the Finger Lakes region in the northwestern part of the state. The first serious producer there is generally credited as Dr. Konstantin Frank of Dr. Frank Cellars on Keuka

Lake. Although he was discredited as crazy or worse in his lifetime (mostly because he wanted to grow Riesling), the good doctor is credited with creating the first serious Finger Lakes wine when he made a sweet Riesling in 1962. Up until then, all the region's winemakers focused on Labrusca or native American hybrid grapes that were cold-weather-hardy if not particularly great.

Examples of these hardy if unthrilling wines include Catawba and Baco Noir—both of which are still grown in the Hudson Valley as well as the Finger Lakes.

Dr. Frank went on to make other wines, sweet and dry and sparkling, over the years—and to inspire another generation of Finger Lakes winemakers who were as quality-minded if not as crazy. Dr. Frank's putative protégé, Hermann Wiemer, founded his own winery and made even better Riesling than his mentor and, in turn, he schooled his own talented protégé, Fred Merwarth, who even ended up buying the Wiemer winery.

There are now at least a dozen notable wineries in the Finger Lakes where first-rate Rieslings are made, as well as a wide range of other whites and reds (with more uneven success). In fact, the Finger Lakes today is a mecca of sorts for aspiring young winemakers thanks to the affordability of its vineyard land (a twentieth the price of Napa), the proximity of Cornell University, and the possibilities of working with a wide range of grapes. Twenty years ago, people talked only in terms of Finger Lakes Riesling, but now winemakers have found success with Gewürztraminer, Chardonnay, Cabernet Sauvignon, and (maybe) even Pinot Noir.

The same is true out on the North and South Forks of eastern Long Island, where diversity is the rule, although the vineyard land is a good deal more expensive owing to its concurrent status as a resort. (It's only two hours from Manhattan.) The husband and wife team (now estranged) of Alex and Louisa Hargrave planted the first vinifera grapes on the North Fork four decades ago, and while their track record was both bad and good, they attracted a number of fellow winemakers who also decided to focus on familiar grapes like Chardonnay, Cabernet, and Merlot.

Other North and South Fork winemakers planted other grapes, too, like Cabernet Franc (sometimes good, sometimes not) Sauvignon Blanc (very successful), Syrah (not so much), and Albariño and Chenin Blanc (my favorite but there's only one Chenin producer, Paumanok Vineyards, so far). On the South Fork, winemaker Christopher Tracy at Channing Daughters Winery has a portfolio full of unexpected varietals (Teroldego, Pinot Grigio, Tocai Friulano) and some very good wines.

But perhaps the greatest accomplishment of all for New York State winemakers is the fact that their wines are now considered not only good but even hip. It's become difficult not to find a few New York wines on a wine list in Brooklyn—that hippest of boroughs. This is something that few New York winemakers could have predicted ten years ago, when many were still struggling to find a market. And no market is tougher or more discerning than New York. It just took time to break through. Billy Joel could probably relate. When he wrote "New York State of Mind" some forty years ago, it wasn't a big hit—it wasn't even released as a single. It took Billy Joel playing it over and over again to make it an audience favorite and eventually even an anthem.

Oxymoron No More

SOME NEW WINE REGIONS ARE "OLD-NEW"; that is, vines may have been planted in a place for a long time but it has also been replanted and revitalized. Other wine regions are "new-new" that is, the land has been planted to vineyards for the very first time. Although the former may have the edge in terms of wine quality, the latter can be even more exciting—if only because it often seems so unlikely.

Take, for example, New Jersey. No state could be more unlikely as a source of high-quality grapes. Tomatoes, perhaps, and asparagus—and of course shopping malls. But *New Jersey* and *good wine* aren't two phrases that are often conjoined.

And yet there are some good wines made in New Jersey—albeit only quite recently and in limited numbers. There are winemakers growing Grüner Veltliner and Syrah and making some pretty good Chardonnays, too. One New Jersey winemaker I met actually left a good winemaking job in Napa for New Jersey. He wanted to be at the beginning of something big and he felt that there was a tremendous potential in the Garden State. He even went one step further, saying the Garden State could rival Napa Valley if only someone would plant the right grapes. (And perhaps tear down a few shopping malls?)

This particular winemaker is employed by a winery situated very close to the New Jersey–Pennsylvania border, about fifty miles from the ocean, although the region is called the Outer Coastal Plain and stretches from one side of the state to another. That's a curious fact of many new winemaking regions—they take up a lot of ground. The OCP (as it's called by its denizens) appellation encompasses more than 2 million acres, and on the OCP website it seems to take up the entire southern half of the state.

There are very few wineries in the OCP right now (about twenty) and they're turning out a wide range of wines—from the good to the very bad—but the region might turn out to be an interesting, even worthy wine destination some years down the road. After all, there have been plenty of wine regions that seemed equally unpromising (Long Island, anyone?). And the OCP has the further advantage of a great acronym.

Who's Keeping Score?

THERE ARE MANY WAYS THAT A WINE IS APPRAISED, but there is only one method that is at once wildly popular and widely scorned. The 100-point rating system that is said to have been first employed by wine critic Robert M. Parker, Jr., and that many critics and publications have since adopted over the years, is brilliant or benighted depending on your philosophy, your sensibility, and even where you live.

For example, if you are a resident of the U.K. you probably feel as many English wine writers do about the 100-point system: many have proclaimed it ludicrous or worse—never mind that many English critics employ their own numerical systems; they just happen to be smaller. Famous English wine critic Michael Broadbent, for example, utilizes a 20-point system.

Some writers use stars to rate wines—a gambit that seems particularly subjective, especially when it comes to half stars. What is the value of half a star? Others employ adjectives in ascending degrees of enthusiasm to rate wines. English wine writer and critic Clive Coates is particularly famous for this; his evaluations include such ratings as Fine, Very Fine, and even Very Fine Plus. Although Mr. Coates also offers excellent and detailed notes on the wines, it seems as if you need to actually know Mr. Coates to understand what was meant by his rating of Very Fine Plus.

The beauty of the 100-point system, as Mr. Parker has explained many times over (other critics may use it but he is the one most often called to defend it), is its simplicity and familiarity. Americans already understood the 100-point system and most had grown up with it in school. (Maybe that is another reason why the English don't like it.) Everyone knew that a score of 90 on a test meant you did pretty well—though not perfectly. An 85 meant there was much room to improve—and a paper that you might want to hide from your parents.

Some people (especially winemakers) disliked the idea that a wine could be reduced to a number. It took away the artistry and the mystery of the experience, they protested—but that was exactly the wine critics' point. A number offered clarity in a way that words like "Very Fine Plus" did not.

And wine retailers loved the numbers too—especially the ones who didn't have the inclination or the wherewithal or the arsenal of adjectives to describe wine with complexity and nuance. The number system was a highly effective selling tool: the higher the number, the easier the sell. And wine writers who awarded high scores saw their names prominently displayed on store shelves—a bit like movie critics whose names are emblazoned on a newspaper ad for a film. There's no better publicity tool for a wine or a critic than a rave.

And that brings me to the 100-point score, the perfect wine. The 100-point scores are particularly irksome to the anti-point crowd. How can someone say they've experienced perfection or, worse, set up the expectation among drinkers that it can be experienced, again and again? I know some wine collectors who will buy only 100-point wines, never mind that the score was awarded at a particular place and time and that Mr. Parker himself has said that a 100-point score was based on "the emotion of the moment" that he had about the wine.

If that's what the numbers really describe—the amount of emotion (read: pleasure) that the wine can provide, perhaps it should be called the 100-point pleasure system. I'd give that name a Very Fine Plus.

Pretty in Pink

I DON'T KNOW MANY WINE DRINKERS WHO TALK—or think—about wine color. Show me a Chardonnay drinker who talks in terms of her wine's golden or green tints or a Cabernet lover who waxes ecstatic over his favored red's garnet hue. But Rosé drinkers are different. They like to look at their wines as much as they like to drink them—perhaps even more.

That may be one reason why Rosé wines are judged by different standards than red and white wines—they're wines for people who are looking for something refreshing and light, of course, but they're also looking for something that looks pretty in a glass. (That's probably one reason why Rosés are assumed to appeal exclusively to women—after all, a man would never invoke the word *pretty*.)

But what makes a Rosé pretty? Which is to say, which color is right? (There are actually color guidelines for Rosés in Provence.) There is a wide range of possible hues: a Rosé can range from pale peach to electric pink to a Rosé so dark it resembles a red. Some of the color will depend on the choice of grape and some will depend on the winemaker's style. For example, a tannic red grape like Cabernet or Syrah is going to create a much darker Rosé than a thin-skinned grape like Pinot Noir. The pigment is in the skin, after all.

It's also a matter of winemaking. A Rosé can be produced by several different methods—skin contact, saignée, and blending—although some methods are officially sanctioned (or forbidden) in certain parts of the world. A skin-contact Rosé is made from red grapes that are crushed and kept in contact with the skins for a few days prior to fermentation. The length of time will help to determine the color of the Rosé.

The saignée (or "bleeding") method calls for removing some of the red wine prior to fermentation, with the leftover wine or juice used to create the pink wine (and a better red wine, too). This makes for a lively if not particularly complicated Rosé. In Provence, where Rosé is the focus, the direct-press method is preferred. This is what is often called an "intentional" Rosé, as the "bleeding" method is often utilized with the red wine first and foremost in mind—the Rosé is often an afterthought. (Provence, by the way, has an entire history of naming the various possible colors of its Rosés—as befits the place that made the wines famous.)

The last method of making a Rosé is illegal in Provence but may be utilized in Champagne and in countries like the United States and Australia: it actually allows for the blending of white wine with red to produce a Rosé. It does sound a bit questionable, but in places like Champagne it's tightly controlled.

Whatever the chosen methodology and whatever the grapes, Rosé is a wine that has become increasingly popular over the years. Rosé sales have soared in recent years and show little sign of slowing. In fact it's almost impossible to find a wine shop that doesn't have a dedicated Rosé section or a restaurant whose wine list doesn't feature at least a few Rosés from various parts of the world. In most cases, they're just lumped together as "Rosés"—never mind if they're made from Grenache or Cabernet or Pinot Noir or in France or Austria. I've only been in one store that arranged their Rosés in exactly the right fashion: by color, from lightest to darkest.

Hold the Sulfites

THE MOST COMMONLY REQUESTED WINE IN ANY WINE SHOP isn't one that is red or white but one that is "sulfite free." Whenever someone reports having a headache after consuming a glass—or a bottle—of wine, they inevitably ascribe it to the presence of sulfites—hence the perennial search for a wine that's free of the substance. Except, of course, that such a wine doesn't actually exist.

Sulfites occur naturally in every wine during the fermentation process and they are almost always added (in the form of sulfur dioxide) prior to bottling. This prevents the wine from oxidizing or spoiling later in life or during transit (the sulfur dioxide a protective layer against the incursion of oxygen, which is the enemy of wine).

There are some wines that have very little added sulfur—some winemakers, especially those who identify themselves as "natural" or "organic," eschew adding much sulfur dioxide, and sometimes they don't add any at all. This can create a different problem—a wine that is less stable and that sometimes ends up oxidizing in the bottle since it doesn't have the protective sulfur dioxide shield. This can make a white wine look and taste like sherry—and a red wine taste dried out and tired.

The fact is that when most people blame an adverse reaction to a wine that they think has a lot of sulfites it's often something else altogether. It's often a wine that's high in alcohol—in fact, this probably causes more headaches than anything else. The second most likely culprit is histamines, which are found in higher amounts in certain types of red wine than others (usually reds with more tannins, like Cabernet or Syrah) and more often in reds than whites. This creates a condition that even has it own acronym: RWH, or red wine headache. (By the way, white wines generally have greater amounts of sulfites than reds.)

There is actually an easy way to determine whether one is truly allergic to histamines or sulfites. For the latter, eat a few pieces of dried apricot, which is high in sulfites. If you don't develop a headache or suffer some other sort of reaction, you're likely not sulfite-allergic. For histamines, eat some pepperoni and salami on a piece of sourdough bread (all high in histamines). If you don't suffer, you're probably fine too.

Another common cause of headaches—perhaps more common than anything else save for overindulgence—is drinking cheap wine. Cheap wines tend to be more manipulated than pricier bottles—sugar may be added to the alcohol to enhance flavor—creating what some would call a less "pure" form of alcohol. This might be the easiest—if possibly the priciest—way to fix the problem.

For anyone who is fearful of an adverse reaction from a glass of wine, here's my advice: spend more, drink less, and steer clear of those big, high-alcohol reds.

Overlooked Alsace

SOME WINE REGIONS DON'T GET THE LOVE THEY DESERVE. While this is true of many places all over the world, it's particularly true of Alsace, France. One reason may be its back-and-forth history. Is it French or is it German? It's been both, many times over. The last time the region changed hands was World War II, when the Germans gave it back, battered and bombed, to the French.

The wines of Alsace offer evidence of that dual identity: although they are French in name, their look is Teutonic. The bottles are the thin, green tapered bottles of Germany, and the grapes—Riesling, Sylvaner, and Gewürztraminer—are German in origin as well. And Alsace wines, again like their German counterparts, are known by grape names, not place names like everywhere else in France. For example, instead of a Macon-Villages, whose unmentioned grape is Chardonnay, the wine would be labeled simply Alsace Riesling, with no mention of a place, unless it was made from a notable (grand cru) vineyard.

Alsace is also a white wine–focused region like the wine regions of Germany—despite the fact that some of its winemakers—like Germans, too—are now keen on making Pinot Noir (with mixed results in both places so far). And finally, the wines of Alsace are fragrant and often off-dry (sometimes unpredictably so), another common German condition, although the Rieslings of Alsace are typically richer than their German counterparts.

Some wines have mysterious names like Edelzwicker and Gentil, which have no counterpart in other parts of France. The former is a word derived from the German (of course) and denotes a wine that is a field blend of various grapes. The second term is a blend as well, but whereas Edelzwicker (the *zwicker* part of the name means "blend") can be composed of almost any grape grown in Alsace, a Gentil wine must contain a minimum amount of Riesling, Gewürztraminer, and/or Muscat.

One clearly French connection is the creation of fifty-one Alsace grand cru vineyards back in 1975. Like the grand cru vineyards of Burgundy, the Alsace grand cru vineyards range in size, and various wine producers may hold different-sized parcels within the same vineyard. But unlike Burgundy, there can be more than one varietal produced in an Alsace grand cru vineyard. For example, in the famed Altenberg vineyard, both Gewürztraminer and Riesling are grown and accorded grand cru status. (Only Chardonnay or Pinot Noir can be grown in a grand cru vineyard in Burgundy.)

Perhaps it's because Alsace combines the complexity of two countries and not just one that Americans are especially confused by the region. In fact, the U.S. sales of Alsace wines have never been particularly strong. But that might be because Alsace wines are made from the grapes that most Americans fear (Riesling, Gewürztraminer).

In any case, the wines of Alsace deserve to be better known in this country—and consumed more often. They are some of the most distinctive, food friendly, and especially aromatically flamboyant wines. In fact, that is one distinction that Alsace can fully claim: it's certainly one of the best-scented wine regions in the world.

Pinot Country

THE STORY OF OREGON is the story of a single grape: Pinot Noir. And it's a story that Oregon winemakers like to tell over and over again. It's the reason for their great success and recognition in the wider wine world.

It is also a story of specialization and something that gives Oregon wine growers a clear identity lacking by growers in other, often less celebrated states. And while other grapes grow well in Oregon (Syrah, Chardonnay, and Pinot Gris), they are almost beside the point. Pinot is king in this monovarietal state.

It's something that Oregon's neighbors to the north seem to half mock and half envy. So many grapes grow well in Washington State, it's hard to have a central identity, Washington winemakers have observed ruefully. And they're right. The range is wide in Washington: Cabernet, Merlot, Sauvignon Blanc, Syrah, Chardonnay, Cabernet Franc, Riesling —they all grow well. But they don't contribute a clear identity.

Of course, Oregon's commitment to Pinot Noir can be a double-edged sword, since Pinot Noir is a highly fickle grape and one that may be challenging to fix one's fortunes upon. It's susceptible to disease and rot, especially when there's a lot of bad weather (and rain). And rain is Oregon's other crop. It rains a lot in Oregon—although I've read that the precipitation is often optimistically described as "Oregon sunshine" by its residents.

But when it rains just enough—and not too much—the Pinot Noir in Oregon can be very good, some say as close to Burgundy as the grape can be in the United States. So close, in fact, that even some Burgundians like Robert Drouhin have built Oregon wineries (Domaine Drouhin) and put down roots.

In fact, many Oregon winemakers with no direct ties to France like to say they make "Burgundian" Pinot Noirs, which admittedly sounds rather pretentious, but they mean that their wines are more subtle, more about minerals and earth, than the Pinot Noirs of California, which they often decry as being "too overt." A good Oregon Pinot is rarely overt. However, when confronted with their inevitable rainy vintages, Oregonians likely wish for the long warm seasons that Californians enjoy.

Oregon Pinot Noir's virtues and value are well established—and the number of its wineries and vineyards simply keeps growing. There are now over five hundred wineries in Oregon making more than 28,000 tons of Pinot Noir (four times the runner-up grape, Pinot Gris, at just over 7,000 tons). Pinot Noir accounts for about half of the wine sales in the state. Whatever the downside might be in specializing in a finicky grape, Oregon hasn't felt it. For the foreseeable future, and for matters of fame and fortune, Pinot Noir is (still) Oregon's most favored grape and greatest specialty.

Great-Aunts and Groovers

THE STEREOTYPICAL TIPPLE OF GREAT-AUNTS EVERYWHERE is the drink of choice for some very hip sommeliers, too. Puzzled as to what that could be? Here's a hint: it's variously preceded by words such as *fino*, *manzanilla*, *palo cortado*, and *amontillado*. While they may sound like dance tunes, they're all types of Sherry.

Sherry is a fortified wine made in the Jerez region of Spain—the name is a bastardized English form, no doubt created by English wine merchants who either didn't know how to pronounce *Jerez* or decided that the wines needed a more "English" sound (especially when they began selling them to wine drinkers back home).

There is only one wine that can legally be called Sherry (as the EU ruled in 1996), although there have been many "Sherries" produced in many places over the years, including California (where some cheap "Sherries" still show up). But these are inevitably low-quality fortified wines whose producers wanted to capitalize on a famous name. True Sherry is made from very specific grapes—Palomino, Pedro Ximenez (aka PX), and Moscatel, aka Muscat. They may be blended or bottled alone as a varietal wine.

A key component of Sherry and what makes the wine unique is flor, a yeast that forms naturally during the winemaking process and covers the wine with a protective shield. It only works as a nonoxidation agent if the wine is between 14.5 and 16.5 percent alcohol—the flor can't survive at a higher level of alcohol.

There are three basic types of Sherry, ranging from dry to sweet. Fino Sherries are the driest and palest because they are protected from oxidation by the flor. They're also the lowest in alcohol. If the alcohol exceeds 16.5 percent—and some Sherries can be as much as 18 percent, the wine will oxidize and it becomes an oloroso Sherry. These Sherries can be dry or sweet, but they're always quite dark—almost the color of molasses—due to their exposure to air. They're also quite full-bodied and rich.

Amontillado is the third type of Sherry, and it's between oloroso and fino in terms of both style and color. The amontillados have a bit of flor protection and a bit of oxidation as well, and their aromas can be quite complex, from nuts to cinnamon to toffee and orange peel—one reason why amontillado is usually the Sherry of preference for soms.

There are other kinds of Sherry; in fact, for a wine with such a simple name there are a bewildering array of types, from cream Sherries (these tend to be cheap, commercial drinks) to manzanilla Sherries (which come from a very specific place near the sea—and are said to smell a bit like it as well) and palo cortado Sherries that are somewhere between an amontillado and an oloroso in character and color.

And for true Sherry mavens, the wines of greatest interest are very old Sherries (VOS) and very old reserve Sherries (VORS). Both these wines are aged for a minimum number of years. They tend to be quite rich as well as expensive—often hundreds of dollars a bottle. (Bodegas Tradición and González Byass both produce highly acclaimed aged Sherries.)

The one last important fact about Sherry is the solera system specific to this wine and this part of the world. (There are other places where the solera system is employed but none as famously as Sherry.) Solera—or "on the ground"—is a blending system whereby wine is moved from barrel to barrel. The barrels are stacked in a tier, with the oldest barrel on the ground. Only a certain amount of the wine in each barrel can be drawn off each year, according to the law.

It means the wines have a consistency of flavor and character—with just enough freshness from the new wine and just enough complexity from the old wine. It's complicated and time-consuming. It's also why there is no such thing as a "vintage" Sherry; all Sherries are a blend of many years.

Sherry is traditionally served in a rather cunning small glass called a *copita* that accommodates a pretty small pour—two and a half ounces (65 mL) versus the standard five ounces (150 mL) for a nonfortified wine. (I'm convinced that the delicate *copita* is one of the reasons that aunts came to like Sherry so much.)

And the sommeliers? Aside from the fact that Sherry can be quite complex in terms of its creation and its many types (and sommeliers hoard complexity like squirrels do nuts), it's the fact that Sherry goes so well with food. From finos to pair with light appetizers (cheeses and olives) to tapas (ham or sardines or even an egg) with amontillados or even olorosos. There is a type of Sherry for just about anything or any occasion.

Some Enchanted Island

I'VE VISITED SICILY ONLY ONCE and I didn't get around the island very much, at least not as much as I'd hoped to. That's because my friend and I traveled largely by train—not an easy way to visit wineries, nor a particularly pleasant transit experience. "No one travels by train in Sicily," one winemaker's wife said to us at one point. "Only the goats." I'm happy to report there were no goats in our compartment and that aside from the train rides my time in Sicily was one of my most memorable Italian wine and travel experiences.

It's been almost seven years since we took our trip and in the intervening years the wines of Sicily have only gotten better and more sought after. One reason has to do with a larger renewed interest in native grapes in Italy overall and in Sicily in particular. These grapes include red varieties like Nerello Mascalese and Nerello Cappuccio as well as Frappato and Nero d'Avola, the most popular red grape.

There has also been increased interest in wines from ambitious quality-minded small producers where once there were only cheap industrial wines from Sicilian co-ops. This is particularly true of the wines made in the Mount Etna region on the island's eastern edge.

In addition to being the home of one of the most active volcanoes in the world—which is still erupting quite regularly (2013 was a very busy year, volcanically)—it's one of the most dynamic winegrowing regions on the island. There is a cadre of producers in the Mount Etna region led by Giuseppe Benanti (more on him in a bit) who are turning out brilliant and savory reds, some of which have been compared to Pinot Noir thanks to their transparency and elegance.

There is no Pinot Noir grown on Mount Etna; the two main red grapes are Nerello Mascalese and Nerello Cappuccio. The former is the grape that is most often compared to Pinot Noir in terms of aromas and textures—and finicky personality, alas. (It's also hard to grow.) Nerello Cappuccio is less important but also less temperamental and is credited with bringing softness and a certain fruity charm where Nerello Mascalese brings complexity and character.

Giuseppe Benanti is the winemaker most often credited with the renaissance of Mount Etna. In fact, when he began making serious wines back in the 1990s, he was almost alone in his endeavor. But when his wines began to receive critical attention, others soon followed, including the 1980s rock star Mick Hucknall, aka Simply Red, whose winery is named, self-referentially, Il Cantante, or "The Singer."

Another well-known and much-heralded Mount Etna winery, Tenuta delle Terre Nere, was created by well-known wine exporter Marc de Grazia, who came from northern Italy but nevertheless decided that Mount Etna was where he wanted to make wine. At Terre Nere (which translates loosely as "farm of the black earth," in honor of the volcanic soils), Mr. de Grazia and company turn out a number of intriguing reds marked by bright acidity and notes of earth and spice, as well as an impressive white and Rosé.

While winemaking is always an uncertain business, it's a particularly uncertain endeavor when it's practiced in some of the highest vineyards in Europe on the side of an active volcano. On the other hand, the volcano has produced some particularly good soils (volcanic soils are rich in calcium, magnesium, and iron). And, of course, Mount Etna is a place that just about everyone in the world has probably heard of (the volcano was constantly in the news in 2013), which surely benefits the marketing campaign.

A Taste of Place

THE MOST OVERUSED WORD IN WINE isn't actually one that anyone can truly define. Created by the French to describe a specific confluence of circumstances under which wine is made, *terroir* may be interpreted as many ways as it is mispronounced. (Say "tear-waa.")

Terroir encompasses geography and geology and climate and plant material, too. It's seen and unseen, the physical and the metaphysical properties of a wine, although the most commonly accepted definition is that *terroir* means "a sense of place." For example, the characteristically chalky soil of Chablis is considered one crucial element of its terroir. Ditto the volcanic soil of Mount Etna in Sicily.

The word *terroir* has become so popular it has also been applied to many other things besides wine. There is cheese with terroir and coffee with terroir. There is even chocolate with terroir (but no, this does not apply to Hershey, Pennsylvania).

Although winemakers—and cheesemakers, coffee growers, and chocolate producers—have a vital role in shaping their products, the terroir of their products is presumed to be a completely natural thing. A wine tastes the way that it does because of a certain place. But it can't just be any old place; only a special place has a true terroir, established over many years, perhaps even centuries. In that sense, history also plays a role in establishing terroir. Something can only show a sense of place if the place itself has proven to deliver noteworthy wines over and over again.

Sometimes wines that are said to have certain terroirs have later been revealed to be wines with faults; what some wine drinkers believed were marks of terroir—funky odors and animal notes—were actually Brettanomyces (wild yeast growth) or cork taint.

Some wine professionals believe this is one reason why the "New World" wine regions (which is to say everywhere outside of Europe) don't really have terroir—it's simply too young. To them terroir also has to have a historical component—of an unspecified number of years. Of course, winemakers from New Zealand to Napa would disagree—especially if they've been making wines somewhere for decades.

Sometimes wines that are made from distinct places are said to possess a *goût de terroir*, or a taste of a specific place (although it is sometimes translated as "taste of the earth"). These are wines that are supposedly so transparent, so powerful, that they directly transmit the vineyard into a glass. But it's a phrase that can also be applied as a fiscal weapon against the unwitting drinker. As an English wine writer once said to me, "When they say goût de terroir—reach for your wallet."

Malbec the Mighty

THERE ARE CERTAIN CHARACTERISTICS that a popular wine should (always) possess. First and foremost, its name must be one that is easy to pronounce. And the wine must be available—pricewise—at both the low and high end. It should be widely available—in serious shops and grocery stores, too. And it should be easy to drink—preferably marked by lots of juicy, ripe fruit.

Is it any wonder Malbec has taken the wine world by storm in recent years? After all, it has every attribute on this list—and more. It's made in a much-romanticized country famous for its tango and gauchos and steak (and government bankruptcies, but never mind those). Indeed, Argentina is considered by many to be the home of Malbec, although the grape actually came from the Cahors region of France.

It was all the way back in the mid-nineteenth century that a French agronomist introduced Malbec to Argentina, and although it took more than a hundred years for it to become popular, it has far outstripped the original French version in terms of visibility and popularity.

Argentine Malbec is very different from that of France. The Malbec of Cahors is a much denser, more tannic, more "serious" wine. Its nickname, "the black wine of Cahors," is well deserved. A Cahors can take years to come around. Argentine Malbec is softer and fruitier and more velvety. It is also much more accessible, though just as dark. It can be quite serious and polished—especially when produced in high-altitude vineyards in and around the Mendoza region (the Napa of Argentina, as it's sometimes known, although its vineyards are considerably higher in altitude).

There is more Malbec grown in Argentina than anywhere else in the world today, although more and more winemakers from other countries, inspired by the Argentine success, have decided to plant it themselves. There is now Malbec in places where one would never expect to find it, like New Zealand, Long Island, and Washington State. These wines have been modestly successful both in terms of wine quality and the marketplace.

But the Argentine version is the grape's great success story. There isn't any country that can come close to producing good wines as reliably, in large volume, and at such a good price. Although some wine pundits have predicted its fall for the past several years (it's the way of all popular grapes, after all), Malbec has maintained its hold on wine drinkers' hearts. Perhaps it has something to do with the tango and steak.

Reading Between the Lines

THERE AREN'T MANY DOCUMENTS that are approached with more trepidation and fear, perhaps even terror, than a restaurant wine list. (Possible exceptions include a prenuptial agreement or a decree of divorce). The reasons range from fear of the unknown (all those wine names) to a fear of the expense (all those zeros next to those names). And, of course, there is the fear of humiliation—from mispronouncing the name of the wine to choosing something terrible.

There isn't anything intrinsically off-putting about wine lists aside from a wealth of type. Most tend to be organized according to the wine's color and place of origin, with all the important countries and regions listed individually and all the ones that don't matter much relegated to the collective category near the end often unimaginably labeled "miscellaneous." (Some sommeliers try to dress this section up a bit and call it something like "Sommelier's Picks" or "Interesting Wines," though both titles do seem to imply that everything else was something the sommelier passed by or didn't find much worth his or her time.)

These wine lists have the appeal of a city whose streets are laid out on a grid: there's the reassurance of a pattern that's repeated over and over again. And yet some sommeliers believe that they're too "narrow" or don't convey enough of the "character" of the wines. So they create wine lists that read more like emotional charts—with categories like "Bold and Daring Reds" or "Soft and Sensitive Whites." Although they were presumably intended

to simplify matters (and to pretend that wine isn't organized by geography everywhere else in the world), these sorts of wine lists are much harder to read. They seem to require some sort of self-examination rather than provoke a discussion of their compatibility with food.

Some wine lists are organized by dollar amounts. I've seen wine lists divided into fiscal subcategories: wines under fifty dollars and wines over fifty dollars and sometimes all wines under a specific dollar amount. This might seem to be useful; at least you know how much you are going to have spend straightaway. On the other hand, the wines are more often than not gathered in a geographic and varietal jumble with nothing more clearly in common than a couple of numbers. At least with a geographically organized wine list it's clear they all come from the same place.

And then there are the fanciful descriptions that often accompany listed wines that I often find only confuse matters further. In fact, I've actually found some wine descriptions so confusing that I've had to ask the sommelier to tell me what he or she meant—and then I still end up asking them to tell me something about the actual wine).

As sales documents go, the wine list is a decidedly imperfect tool. (And that's all a wine list is: a sales prospectus from owner to buyer.) It's why a talented salesman with a palate (aka a sommelier) is required to interpret and guide. So the next time, should you feel intimidated or overwhelmed by a wine list, remember: you're in charge. Tell the sommelier how much you are willing to spend or point to a wine and say something to the effect of "this is what I had in mind." A good sommelier will know you mean both type and price. A wine list, after all, is just a sales tool to use exactly how and when you like.

Loire Valley Love

THE FIRST TIME I VISITED THE LOIRE VALLEY IN FRANCE, it reminded me of Ohio. (Save for the architecture, of course—ranch houses in France are far outnumbered by châteaux. Is there even a French word for *ranch house*?) But the verdant green and gentle hills of the Loire landscape reminded me a bit of the best parts of that midwestern state. And the wines themselves weren't at all bad.

I've been in love with the wines of the Loire Valley for a very long time—many years prior to that first visit. My first love was Pouilly-Fumé, a wine that was once actually more famous than Sancerre (a long time ago). Both are made from Sauvignon Blanc but on opposite sides of the Loire River; Pouilly-Fumé is a bigger, richer, and muskier wine than Sancerre, which tends to be more citrusy and bright.

Pouilly-Fumé was probably famous because a lot of people confused it with Pouilly-Fuissé, another wine that was hot back in the '70s. Never mind that Pouilly-Fuissé was not made from Sauvignon Blanc or in the Loire but was rather a Chardonnay from Burgundy. (Both have faded quite a bit since their heyday.)

Sancerre, on the other hand, keeps getting bigger and bigger. It's a wine that sommeliers can't keep in stock. Some won't even serve it by the glass because their diners won't order anything else. Sancerre is surely one of the greatest success stories of the Loire. The wines are more of a mixed bag. Some Sancerres are intensely minerally, while others are taut to light and crisp, and some are simply forgettable, depending on where the wines are made, by whom, and the profit margin he or she might have in mind.

While Sancerre is one of the most famous wines of the Loire and, some might argue, its most overpriced (popularity does that), there are many underpriced wines in the Loire. In fact, it may be home to some of the best bargains in France. I can think of half a dozen underpriced Loire wines—both red and white—off the top of my head.

Muscadet would be at the top of this list. This crisp white wine of the far western edge of the valley (near Nantes) is the pluperfect shellfish and aperitif wine. And yet the best examples from the best producers rarely cost more than fifteen dollars a bottle—a number that hasn't shifted in years. (And a reason why so many Muscadet growers have gone broke, alas.)

The winemakers of Vouvray—an appellation in the middle of the Loire—are doing better financially, but their wines are still underpriced for their quality and diversity. Vouvray, a white wine made from the Chenin Blanc grape, can be sparkling, still, and sweet. And it ages wonderfully too.

The Loire options and possibilities go on and on—the Chinons (reds) made from the Cabernet Franc grape are generally charming and lithe, while the Bourgueil reds (also Cabernet Franc) tend to be a bit more rustic and rich. There are both reds and whites from the region of Saumur (also famous, incidentally, for its riding academy), where they also make an excellent sparkling wine that many budget-minded French men will drink instead of Champagne.

It's been a very long time—many hundreds of years—since the wines of the Loire Valley were held in great esteem by the world. (It once outstripped Bordeaux in terms of prestige.) Now its wines are appreciated primarily by savvy wine professionals and budget-minded connoisseurs. And wine journalists, too.

The Truth About Vintages

ONE OF MY FAVORITE MAXIMS WAS COINED by the man whose name is shorthand for genius. "Never memorize anything you can look up," Albert Einstein once counseled—and I've spent a great deal of time doing just that.

Memorization is a skill that every wine lover should possess—and there is a lot of memorization to be done when it comes to wine. There are the names of the most important producers, the top wineries, domaines, and châteaux, as well as the wines, winemaking regions, and thousands of different grape varieties.

But most of all, there are the vintages. Any oenophile worth his or her weight in Mouton Rothschild is expected to know at least some of the best and the worst vintages of the past several years, if not the past several decades. And the responsibility goes back even further in time when it comes to regions like Burgundy and Bordeaux, whose greatest vintages have been catalogued for hundreds of years.

And yet very few nonprofessional wine drinkers I know talk about wine in terms of vintages. They never ask if a certain year was great or compare one vintage of wine to another. They definitely don't ask if a wine is "ready to drink." (Certain wines in certain vintages are more pleasurable to drink later rather than sooner.)

Of course that may be because almost all wines are ready to drink once they're in the market (95 percent is a conservative estimate), and so the possession of vintage knowledge is practically moot. In fact, it's probably much more useful to memorize names than numbers—as the old saying goes, a good vintner can make a good—or at least drinkable—wine even in bad times.

On the other hand, I can't say it hasn't been useful to know good vintages from bad when the producers' names are unknown to me. (How many times have you picked up a wine list without seeing a single familiar name?) Knowing, for example, that 2010 was an excellent year in Burgundy (particularly for whites) has emboldened me to choose a white Burgundy from that year made by a producer I'd never heard of but in a vintage I thought might be pretty good.

When a vintage is a resounding success—that is, the conditions were just right for ripening grapes—even bad winemakers (of which there are fewer and fewer thanks to better winemaking and viticultural techniques) can make a passable wine. And there are far fewer numbers to know than there are winemakers' names. (Even if you kept track of several vintages in ten major winemaking regions in the world you'd be ahead of the game.)

And then there's the pleasure of memorization itself. As any poetry lover or sports fan can attest, there is pleasure in keeping lots of verse—or stastistics—in your head. The importance of wine vintages is actually the importance of memorization—the value of learning and remembering. After all, we can't all be geniuses like Einstein, who didn't bother to memorize much of anything because he was making up his own brilliant theorems instead.

It's Easy Being Green

EVEN MY SERIOUS WINE COLLECTOR FRIENDS drink a few nonserious wines from time to time. For one friend, it's Sancerre, which he calls his "pool wine" even though he hasn't owned a pool in years.

One of my favorite nonserious wines is Vinho Verde. It's even simpler than a pool wine—it's more like a dash through the sprinkler. There's not much in the middle or in the end of it—but in the beginning Vinho Verde is wonderfully bright.

Vinho Verde, the so-called green wine of Portugal, is light and a bit frothy and spritzy (either naturally or through a bit of added carbonation), but with good acidity it's low alcohol too—often lower than 10 percent. You can drink an entire bottle of Vinho Verde and not feel its effects. And you won't feel the cost of its purchase, either; a bottle of

Vinho Verde costs as little as five dollars—although there are more "serious" ones (a relative term) that can cost ten dollars or more.

These are the more minerally textural wines made from the Alvarinho grape (Portugal's equivalent of Albariño over in Spain) instead of a blend of grapes like Loureiro, Trajadura, Azal Branco, and Pedernã, which produce lighter, slighter wines.

Vinho Verde is made in the Minho region of northwest Portgual and it's the largest wine appellation in the country—a bit sprawling and unkempt, just like its vines. Indeed, the grapevines of Vinho Verde were once trained to climb up on fences and poles, squeezed into spaces rather nicely laid out on wires. There are a lot of vines in random-seeming places—it looks like everyone in Vinho Verde is making wine. This has changed a bit over time, and most vines in Vinho Verde are now arranged in an orderly fashion and look just like those in any other wine country.

The one caveat to Vinho Verde is that it needs to be consumed in its youth—perhaps more especially than any other wine in the world as its charms are decidedly fleeting. And while Vinho Verde doesn't come with an expiration date like a beer, it does come with a bottling date that can usually be found on the back label, although sometimes it's in a code that can be hard to interpret by anyone who doesn't work at the winery. That's the only complicated aspect of Vinho Verde—everything else is easy.

The Long View

WHO WILL BE THE NEXT BIG NAME IN WINE? What will be the next great wine region, the up-and-coming appellation, or the break-out grape? Will Pinot Noir ever fade from view? Could there even be a second coming of Merlot? These are the sorts of questions that can keep wine writers and their editors—and even some wine merchants and sommeliers—awake at night. They all have to keep abreast of the trends and have all the right wines—or they will have to make them up.

Most casual wine drinkers have only a passing interest in this sort of crystal ball stuff; more often than not, they're happy to drink the wines they know or that their friends or wine merchants recommend. They don't want—or need—to know that Roter Veltliner is cool and Chardonnay is passé. (At least to some people.)

Why are so many people in the wine trade so focused on trends? Isn't that something best left to the fashion business? After all, winemakers can't rip out a non-trendy vineyard the way a seamstress might a too-low hem, only to replant it with another trendy grape when that particular trend ends.

The business of grape growing is an investment of time as much as money; it takes several years for a new vineyard to produce decent-quality fruit. Some vineyard managers might even wait as long as five years to harvest from a new vineyard. Of course, others might resort to the quick fix of grafting—when a different varietal is grafted onto an existing rootstock of another—like Cabernet Sauvignon grafted onto Sauvignon Blanc. But grafting can be risky—if you follow a trend, it might just turn out to be one with a sudden end.

Although wine drinkers should definitely experiment as much as possible, trying as many different types of wines from as many types of places as they can, it's never a good idea to drink or to follow what someone somewhere has decided is "hot." Aside from the unattractive idea of "group think," if you're drinking a wine at the time that it's perceived as the "in" thing it probably means that the wine, like a hot stock, is probably overvalued—and hence overpriced.

A wine made with care probably won't ever be "fashionable." Wine is an agricultural product, after all, formed not by fashion or trends but weather and circumstance—and a winemaker's hard work.

Glass Warfare

THERE ARE CERTAIN THINGS ABOUT WINE that I truly dislike. A list of the worst would include pretension, high prices, and wines by the glass. The first two are largely indefensible, while the third actually has quite a few fans. I know a lot of people who think that the service of wines by the glass in a restaurant is one of the great populist tools. "So many options! So many opportunities to sample a wine!" these by-the-glass cheerleaders exclaim.

Instead, I simply regard a wine by the glass as a restaurant's great profit center. After all, standard by-the-glass pricing calls for one glass to equal the cost of the bottle, and there are five glasses of wine in a standard bottle of wine—although some restaurants will get only four due to generous pouring practices or simple waste.

But the profit center pricing isn't my only objection to wines by the glass, nor is the fact that some restaurants will purposely—or accidentally—offer what is known in the business as a "short pour": less than the promised five- or six-ounce-glass offering. (I have actually been to restaurants whose by-the-glass wines are a mere four ounces—which means they get six glasses of wine out of the bottle.)

No, my biggest argument isn't actually monetary but sensory in nature. A bottle of wine utilized for by-the-glass pours can be left open for days—in fact, I've been to restaurants where the by-the-glass bottles have been open as a long as a week. This doesn't give the drinker a very good impression of the wine if they happen to order a glass on day five. And I don't believe that any preservation system can keep a five-day-old wine in the same shape as a just-opened bottle. An open bottle is immediately compromised.

Add to that the fact that a waitress or bartender rarely seems to know how long the bottle has been open and often doesn't much care. For example, I've even witnessed the latter pouring out the dregs of one bottle into a glass and mixing it with a bit of a fresh bottle. After all, it's not the wine but the profit that's inside the glass.

I once proposed to a restaurateur that he price his wines by the glass according to the time that the bottle was open. For example, if a wine cost fifteen dollars a glass the day the bottle was first opened, it should cost twelve the following day and nine the third day and so on until the wine was free—or it was gone. He thought the idea had merit but declared it a "logistical nightmare" for his accountants and his bartenders.

He had a point. A bartender who would blend old and new wines in the same glass and serve it probably wasn't the person to be figuring out how many days the wine was open and how much a customer should be charged. But as far as I was concerned, it was another good argument against drinking by-the-glass wines.

Get Smart

WHAT'S THE BEST WAY TO LEARN ABOUT WINE? It's a question that almost every budding oenophile (eventually) asks. And it's a hard question to field—there are so many options today. There are books and videos and tastings at restaurants and stores. A lot of wine merchants have even created their own "education centers," wisely realizing that an educated customer is one who will likely spend a lot more.

There are schools where you can obtain certification or even degrees. Some "schools" may last only a few days or several months and some even offer four-year degrees—although these are usually university programs in viticulture or oenology.

The fact is, most people in search of a wine education only want to know a few things, just enough to keep from feeling—or, more important, sounding—stupid. This might include some basic grape names and facts and key regions as well as information about certain flavors and aromas. A great number of people have told me that they just wanted to know enough to be able to talk to a sommelier. (They didn't specify for how long.)

I've witnessed all forms of wine education over the years. I've audited classes run by well-meaning amateurs and credentialed professors and I've even done a bit of wine "educating" myself, although I put that verb in quotation marks since the seminars and tastings that I conducted were rarely very long and not terribly serious—as much entertainment as education. The truth is that there's not a lot of education that can be acquired by tasting a few wines in a short period of time.

A proper wine education requires years and years of serious application and study. It's all-encompassing and it never ends. Just as soon as you learn something about a wine it's likely to change. Wine is something that can't be understood with books alone and seminars and flash cards but has to be acquired in context and real life—by drinking it, preferably in the company of others.

In that way, learning about wine is a lot like learning a language. You can read books and take classes and perhaps pick up some names and a few helpful phrases ("How much does that cost?" "Where is the restroom?"), but you can't expect to have much insight into a culture or a very interesting exchange if you stop there. You need a context for what you've learned and you must practice it every day. Fortunately, in the case of wine, that means drinking it every day as opposed to practicing the subjunctive of French verbs.

Technically Speaking

WINEMAKERS ARE DETAIL ORIENTED BY NATURE or necessity and most often both. There is much information to track in the making of a wine—from the biological to the meteorological. This isn't information winemakers necessarily want to keep to themselves. Sometimes they'll put it on a back label and sometimes they'll put it on a so-called tech sheet available to curious and (particularly serious) winery visitors. Here's what you might find included in such a document.

Vineyard notes

How many acres, how small or large, is the vineyard? What is the elevation and where is it located? On the side of a mountain or on the valley floor? And what about the type of clones? How well suited are they to the vineyard location? (Certain grapes like Pinot Noir have all types of clones, and some do better in certain kinds of sites than others.)

Vintage notes

How was the weather? Did it rain? Did it hail? Did it do a little of both? And when in the growing season did the rain come? Was it the spring or the fall and did it help or hinder? Was the weather "cooperative" or "challenging" (to use winemakers' words)?

Varietal information

If the wine is a blend of several grapes, winemakers like to give precise percentages. I have no idea why they do this unless it's because wine professionals ask them so much they decided to put it on a piece of paper:

This wine was made of exactly 89 percent Cabernet Sauvignon, 9 percent Cabernet Franc, and 2 percent Petit Verdot. (How much of it is true anyway? 89 Cab versus 91 percent?)

Barrel aging and fermentation

Barrels cost money, so winemakers like to talk about them a lot. Sometimes they will offer details as to what the barrels looked like during fermentation (open or closed) and how many barrels were used or new. (This is also sometimes cited in percentages, too.)

Length of fermentation

The primary fermentation of a wine turns its sugar into alcohol. How long did it take? It depends on the wine and the winemaker's style—and often the yeast that the winemaker employs. Fermentation can last from five to fourteen days—it can also get stuck if the temperature isn't just right—it can't be too high or too low (this is one reason to keep it—as some red winemakers choose—"short and hot").

Barrel maker

Sometimes the cooperage (the barrel-making facility) gets a plug, particularly if it's a fancy (read: expensive) name like François Frères. It shows that this winery really ponied up.

Winemaker

This is where the winemaker's name officially appears—even though he or she may be cited throughout all of the previous notes.

Production

How many bottles or cases did they make of this wine?

Total acidity

The first of the three numbers that matters. Total acidity indicates how much acidity is in the wine—whether it might be too tart (acidity of 1.0 percent) or rather flat (.4 percent). The average acidity of a red wine is around .6 percent, and white wine is a touch higher. If you like a wine with lots of acidity look for the larger number.

The wine's pH

The pH number of a wine will tell you the amount of acidity in a wine (a low-pH wine, say 2.9, has a high acidity) and its stability, too. A wine with a high pH can taste flat and characterless. It can also be unstable (a high pH level, say 3.9, can encourage microbial growth, infecting and in effect ruining the wine).

Alcohol content

This number is the easiest of all three for the budding oenophile to understand. A lower-alcohol wine (Mosel Riesling, Vinho Verde) will be about 7 percent alcohol, while an average wine will be around 12 percent (the numbers keep creeping up). Anything over 14.2 percent alcohol is considered high—and is actually taxed at a higher rate by the U.S. government as well. These numbers are rarely exact, and can be considered accurate if they are within a percentage point.

Lost in Translation

THERE ARE REASONS WHY CERTAIN WINES become popular—
and reasons why certain wines never will. Take, for example, Moscato.
It became the best-selling wine in this country thanks to a sweet profile
and the love of rap stars, and although German Riesling can be sweet and
could even pair nicely with lobster, it will likely never appear in a rap song.

German Riesling is one of the most profound wines in the world—
sommeliers everywhere sing its praises and its versatility with food. I've
never met a sommelier who doesn't claim to be madly in love with the
Riesling of Germany. They love its crystalline acidity, its lovely ripe fruit,
its beguiling aromas (peach, citrus, and apricot), and the fact that it's low
in alcohol. They love its long history (Riesling has been cultivated in
Germany for hundreds of years), and visiting somms love the postcard-
perfect views in the vineyards; some Riesling vineyards are so steep the
grape pickers practically have to crawl on their hands and knees.

But even the most powerful and impassioned cadre of sommeliers
can't do much to address its inherent problem: the names of most German
Rieslings aren't easy to spell or to pronounce. Unlike the French word
cru or the Italian *riserva*, which look so alluring on labels, German wine
words look downright scary. (All those umlauts.)

And there's all the information. German wine producers seem to
feel it's their duty to include every fact—no matter how small or large.
And so they'll cram the name of the estate, the vineyard, the town, the
grape, and when it was picked on the front label.

That last note has to do with the German wine classification system, which references the ripeness of grapes. Unlike wines that are designated grand or premier cru in Burgundy or by classifications of estates as

in Bordeaux, German wines are classified by the Prädikat system of grape ripeness. (There are estates in the Rheingau region that have been designated as "Erstes Gewächs"—the equivalent of a grand cru—but it's not applicable in other regions of Germany.)

There are some German producers who have tried to make their typefaces friendly. They've even added the word *dry* to their name to improve the odds of an American buying their wine. But gaining more non-German drinkers will likely remain a climb uphill. And not just for the reasons I've cited, but also because German Rieslings aren't seen as fashionable or cool (except to those somms).

Maybe German wine needs someone famous to buy a vineyard in the Mosel. Perhaps Angelina Jolie and Brad Pitt, having purchased and improved an estate in Provence, can do their part to make German wine hot.

Zin Again

WHITE ZINFANDEL. Those two words together represent one of the most popular wines of modern times and a phenomenon so powerful that it transformed *blush* from a verb to an adjective. It also made it difficult for producers of (real) red Zinfandel to have their wines taken seriously by the world.

And yet, in more recent history, white Zinfandel was produced in an effort to make a better red Zinfandel. (What history isn't complete without an ironic footnote?) As the legend goes, Zinfandel grower Bob Trinchero, of Sutter Home Winery in Napa, was trying to make a more concentrated red (back in 1972) when he pressed out a bit of the (white) juice and bottled the resulting wine.

He wanted to call it "Oeil de Perdrix" after a Swiss Rosé, but the name was rejected by the Federal Alcohol Administration so he settled on "white Zinfandel." Unwittingly the feds did Mr. Trinchero a great favor, as it's hard to imagine that Oeil de Perdrix, or "Eye of the Partridge," would have resonated with millions of fans quite the same way that white Zinfandel did.

The first few hundred cases of the original white Zins were actually fairly dry wines; the sweeter—and pinker—version came later when Mr. Trinchero, once again by accident, made a sweet version. This was said to have been caused by a "stuck" fermentation—which means there was a bit of residual sugar left when the wine stopped fermenting. The result was a soft, fruity, fairly low-alcohol white (actually pink) that became wildly popular and the source of a small fortune for Mr. Trinchero and Sutter Home.

The wines that followed from Sutter Home's competitors were also called white Zinfandel or more commonly "blush" wines on account of their pinkish peachy glow. There was seemingly no end to Americans' appetite for these sweetish wines—and just about every winery in California soon had its own blush bottling.

The further irony of the white Zinfandel story is that in the end the wine actually saved Zinfandel from possible extinction—or at least a severe reduction of its vineyards. When Mr. Trinchero made that first white Zinfandel, the old Zin vineyards in Napa and Amador Counties and parts beyond were in danger of being ripped out and replanted because they weren't considered commercially viable. But with the advent of white Zinfandel, winemakers were looking to buy the grapes again.

In the ensuing few decades, demand for white Zinfandel has faded a bit (although it still sells quite well) and red Zinfandel is having something of a renaissance, especially the old vine Zinfandels of Napa and the Dry Creek Valley of Sonoma. Even old vine Zinfandel from Lodi—a hot region north of Modesto best known as the home of the grocery store brands like Woodbridge—has become highly prized. Well-known Zinfandel producers from other regions in California like Ravenswood and Joel Gott are turning out Lodi-labeled wines that are also well priced.

Will this latter-day Zinfandel surge last long enough to remove any lingering memories of all that blush? There is at least more reason to hope that Zinfandel will once again be valued even respected—and, most important, be thought of as red.

The Multi-Faceted Glass

I HAVE ONLY ONE TYPE OF WINE GLASS IN MY HOUSE. It's an all-purpose handmade Zalto glass from Austria that I use for every wine that I drink—from Chardonnay to Cabernet, Sauvignon Blanc to Syrah. I use it for Champagne as well, although I do have Champagne flutes that I never use. (Since I no longer use them, they no longer count.) I don't have the shelf space, the money, or, the belief that it's necessary to own lots of different glasses. And the Zalto is not only one of the best-functioning glasses I've found in my years of tastings, it's quite beautiful too.

My father was in the glass business for decades and there was a constant flow of wine glasses into our house. They came from all over the world—Poland, Germany, Ireland, Finland, and, of course, the U.S. My father would probably be appalled that I settled for just a single glass—not because he had strict thoughts about wine but because he loved glassware so much. He liked all types of glasses, actually—how they caught the light and how they felt in your hand. My father wasn't just in the business of marketing glassware. He was singularly glassware-obsessed. He enjoyed a good wine but it was the wine glass that he loved.

Most wine professionals I know think about wine glasses not in terms of their beauty but their functionality. How well do they convey the flavors and aromas of a particular wine? And how well do they resist breakage too, of course.

The Austrian-based Riedel glass company has made a sizable fortune based on the notion that all wine drinkers need all kinds of grape-specific glassware. Actually they don't just make grape-specific glasses, but country-specific glasses as well. Federico Lleonart, an Argentine wine ambassador, once told me that Riedel's Argentine Malbec glass "would not work" for a Malbec produced in Cahors, France. The French Malbec did not have the same qualities as a Malbec from South America, he maintained. The wines were too different and thus each needed its own glass.

It all had to do with the shape of the glass, said Mr. Lleonart. "The shape of the glass directs the flow of the wine. For example, a Pinot Noir glass tips the wine toward the front of your mouth. You don't get as much acid and you get more fruity flavors." That was a good thing with Pinot Noir, which has a lot of fruity flavors, said Mr. Lleonart, but a bad thing with Malbec, which "tends to flatten out" in a Pinot Noir (aka Burgundy) glass. But how many people are truly going to notice, or care, if their Malbec "flattens out" in their non-Malbec glass?

I'd like to ask my father what he thinks of this sort of stuff but he's had trouble remembering things lately. He's even stopped drinking wine, although I don't think he misses it. But I know he misses all those beautiful glasses.

The Pitfalls of Pretending

YOU KNOW THE TYPE: the people who mispronounce the name of a famous wine or make up stories about all the great vintages they've enjoyed. These are what are know in oenological circles as the wine fakers. Their type of pretending might take the form of vague descriptions of shadowy estates or vintages that were never really made, and the best wine fakers sprinkle in a bit of plausible-sounding information to sound almost true. It's a particularly male trait (although there are exceptions—see below).

Why do they do it? What are they hoping to gain? (Or not to lose?) Is it because they think that everyone knows less (or more) about wine than they do? Is it because wine is something that sounds (to them) like it could be just a lot of made-up words?

"This wine is really smooth" is a favorite of a budding wine faker—or, slightly better: "This wine drinks really well"—another kind of say-nothing phrase. Sometimes it's a flat-out lie made by a professional, like the one my friend was treated to at a restaurant in New York.

The place was well respected, somewhat famous for its wine program. My friend ordered an Alsace Gewürztraminer, but it was out of stock. When my friend expressed dissatisfaction, the sommelier quickly assured him that she had a wine that was almost identical.

That wine turned out to be a Sauvignon Blanc. As any wine drinker knows, those two grapes have almost nothing in common. Clearly the sommelier was lying or bluffing—but why? The problem with faking wine knowledge—or faking anything —is that the minute someone who knows something asks you more than a few questions, you're sunk.

This is not to say I haven't faked a wine fact myself. Many, many years ago when I was just starting out in the wine business, I faked having tasted a vintage of a particular wine. I'd had the wine several times but never from that particular year. It was only later that I found that they never made a wine in that particular year.

My fakery wasn't uncovered (until now), as the people around me were even more ignorant, but I decided then and there that I would never fake anything (at least about wine) ever again. Better to be an ignoramus any day than a fraud.

Land of New Discoveries

THERE IS A PHRASE that wine writers were fond of invoking in recent years when describing the state of winemaking in Spain, and I've read it over and over (and over) again: "The sleeping giant has awoken." (Try Googling those words and see if I'm right.) Spain, the purported slumbering vinous beast, is said to have risen out of its decades-long torpor (which is to say, a very long production of plonk) and has started to turn out some quality stuff, though the image that this particular phrase evokes has always been more Fay Wray and King Kong than Rioja and the Priorat.

Those two Spanish wine regions exemplify what "the new Spain" (a more dignified moniker than "the sleeping giant") represents. On the one hand, there is the great traditional winemaking of Rioja, and on the other hand, there is the Priorat, perhaps recently and the most widely heralded.

But these are only two examples: there are a lot of exciting, well-made wines from regions all over Spain. They're bright, juicy white wines made in small regions like Rueda and toothsome reds from sprawling regions like Castilla–La Mancha. They're turned out by cooperatives and tiny boutique bodegas. They're red, white, sparkling, and fortified, made from grapes that everyone knows, like Chardonnay, and grapes like Godello that only wine geeks can pronounce. (Say "go-daY-O.")

A great many of these wines are versatile—easy to drink and friendly with food. They are also very affordably priced. In fact, Spanish wines are some of the most affordable high-quality wines in the world today, with a wide range of options for less than fifteen dollars a bottle. Perhaps "Spain the sleeping giant" would actually be better described as "Spain the Goliath of good deals."

156

Take Your Wine's Temperature

WHEN IS THE LAST TIME YOU TOOK YOUR WINE'S TEMPERATURE? Did you hold the bottle in your hands and consider that it might be too cold—or worse, a little too warm?

One of the most crucial—and most readily overlooked—aspects of wine service and storage is the temperature. This is especially true of bottles stocked in restaurants and stores where there may be little concern for the wines' long-term health. When the temperature is excessively elevated, the wine will age more rapidly. That means that the bottle you may have purchased only a few days ago will taste many years older than it should. A couple of weeks in a too-hot store or restaurant shelf will have an immediate aging effect.

Or if it's really hot, the wine could effectively "cook," all the fruit and acidity baking away. That's what happens when it gets really, really hot inside a shop—or the trunk of a car. But the most common place where too-hot wines are found is, ironically, on a wine delivery truck. A remarkable number of trucks used to transport wine aren't refrigerated, even in the summer months.

Even if it's not cooked or prematurely aged, the mere sensation of a too-warm wine is unpleasant. Tepid is not a word favorably associated with wine. A red that is too warm (over 65 degrees) tends to taste only of alcohol and tannin, while a too-warm white will taste like alcohol and flabby fruit. The acidity will simply evaporate along with the clarity and definition of the fruit.

The fastest way to counteract this effect is to put ice cubes in your glass of wine (white or red) and stir them around for four seconds, then take them out (try not to let them melt in the glass). The late, great wine writer Alexis Bespaloff named four seconds as the proper amount of time—and I named this trick after him, labeling it, sensibly enough, "The Alexis Bespaloff Four-Second Rule."

The opposite, but less troublesome, problem is a wine that is excessively cold. Excess cold (temperatures below 50 degrees) won't ruin a wine; in fact it can help to preserve it. (Cold slows the aging process.) Unless the wine is so cold it's frozen—and even then it's better to freeze a wine than to overheat it. And a cold wine can be readily warmed up. Cup the glass between your hands or maybe put the (unopened!) bottle under your arm for a few minutes. But do not, under any circumstances, put the wine in a microwave—something I've actually seen done.

In the end, I'd always choose a too-cold wine over a wine that was excessively hot. After all, you can raise your body temperature just by raising a glass.

The Biggest Wine Myth

ONE OF THE BIGGEST LIES IN WINE is perpetuated daily by hundreds and perhaps even thousands of wine drinkers. It consists of four simple words: Drink What You Like. It sounds reasonable enough: after all, you wouldn't tell someone to eat something they couldn't abide (unless you were that someone's parent or spouse). And yet "Drink what you like" is actually a terrible piece of advice.

Wine is about exploration and experimentation. It's a beverage of immense variety of flavor, texture, and style. While wine drinking should always be pleasurable, it shouldn't be the same pleasure experienced the same way over and over again. And that's what people often do when they're told to drink what they like. Drink what you like practically guarantees an unadventurous wine-drinking life. How would you discover, for example, that you like a Welschriesling from Moravia if you never try one?

I realize the idea behind this piece of advice is to reassure nervous would-be oenophiles intimidated by an overabundance of choices. But why should anyone be protected from choice? Isn't choice something we all desire?

My counsel instead would be, "Drink what you don't know," and do it over and over again. Take a week out of every month to drink a wine or wines that you've never encountered before. Ask friends, wine merchants, and perfect strangers (with good palates, of course) for recommendations. If you like Chardonnay, drink Pinot Blanc or Pinot Gris and then go on to Garganega (the grape of Soave). Go all the way down the alphabet to Zierfandler—a white grape of Austria.

Wine is a bit of a (calculated) risk that can bring great reward, and there's a pretty limited downside if it doesn't work out. And the more you experiment, the greater your credibility as a drinker when you declare, "I know what I like."

We can't actually smell a wine as well as a dog or a cat or even a possum, but at least we're much better at holding a glass.

Who Knows?

A Vinous Fairy Tale

THE VERY FIRST GAVI I EVER TASTED had a portrait of a princess on the label. I was only twenty-one years old at the time, and this picture was a big selling point. It looked like the wine was made by a royal family. Never mind that the actual wine was rather light bodied and simple; because of that label and the wine's rather wonderful name—Principessa Gavia Gavi—it became "my wine" for a time and I drank it at every opportunity, which was often. And then it abruptly disappeared.

I fell in love with Gavi in the late 1980s, about the same time as everyone else in this country was falling in love with Gavi as well. A simple white wine from the Piedmont region of Italy made from the Cortese grape, Gavi became fashionable because its producers knew about marketing—probably more than they did about winemaking, in fact. Very few of those wines were very good. In fact, Gavi of those days could be called the Pinot Grigio of Piedmont; it was that easy to drink—and to pronounce.

One Gavi producer, La Scolca, was particularly savvy to the potential snob appeal of the wine and, just as Ralph Lauren added a sleak black label to his existing blue and purple labels, the La Scolca producers made both a white-label and a black-label line. The black label was, of course, the more coveted of the two. It wasn't uncommon to hear wine drinkers at the time ask for "the black-label Gavi" in restaurants and stores. The La Scola Gavi dei Gavi is twice the price of the white label. It's made from old vines and aged on its lees, which means it's a little bigger and a little richer than the white-label wine, which, like most Gavis, was a pretty neutral drink.

Gavi has gotten much better over the years—the wines are more concentrated, the producers more ambitious—and yet as a category it has faded away. But when I went looking for Principessa recently, I found a bottle on a grocery store shelf, looking more modern, more ordinary, and, well, cheap. I prefer to think of the wine that I first loved—and the story that inspired the label.

There was once a Princess Gavi in the sixth century who married a commoner despite the objections of her father, the king. Somewhere along the line, the couple drank some of the local wine and they liked it, and when her father found out about their marriage he actually decided to forgive them. Centuries ago in Gavi, the story mattered more than the wine. Even today, not much has changed.

The Wine Aisle

MILLIONS OF WINE DRINKERS BUY BOTTLES IN SUPERMARKETS but I'm not among them (at least not more than a few times a year). My reasons are both practical and emotional. The practical part has to do with the fact that until recently I lived in New York where it's illegal to sell wine in grocery stores. The emotional part is that it simply feels odd. Wine and dish soap? Wine and dog food? They don't seem to belong in the same shopping cart.

And then there is the matter of the wines on the shelves. Most of the wine sold in grocery stores, with a few exceptions, of course, is fairly unexciting stuff. It's mostly quite decent but almost never thrilling. And the identifier alone is off-putting. Does anyone want to buy—or produce—a bottle of "grocery store wine"?

But my biggest objection to wines in supermarkets has to do with the service you get while shopping there. I've rarely found available someone who is able to make a recommendation. There aren't wine experts prowling the aisles of supermarkets as there are in wine stores; no people who have tasted every wine and can tell one vintage from another and which producer is really doing something great. A great wine shop is staffed with people with deep knowledge and love for the products.

Some grocery stores do have people in the wine aisle offering to help, and I've met a few over the years. For example, the Kroger grocery store near my sister's house in suburban Dallas had a very nice woman who offered to help but admitted that she hadn't tasted most of the wines that she was selling. She made recommendations—of a sort—citing wineries she had "heard" were good.

Hearsay may be good enough if you're choosing one brand of butter over another, or a type of dog kibble, but it's not sufficient for me when buying a wine that I know nothing about. In that particular Kroger I ended up buying a few bottles: an Oregon Pinot Noir from a decent producer, an Argentine Malbec that I'd had before, and a New Zealand Sauvignon Blanc from the many New Zealand Sauvignons on the shelf. (Since this is a very popular category in supermarkets, it's here you can find some of the better deals because the turnover is frequent.) The wine salesperson said, "Let me know how it tastes." Was it a casual comment or a plea for enlightenment? I wasn't sure, but I found it depressing to say the least.

I have found truly knowledgeable supermarket wine sales-people in exactly one city: Birmingham, Alabama. I'd traveled there several years back to check out the food and wine scene, then discovered there wasn't a single sommelier in town but there were some wine-savvy people in supermarkets. (I'd been tipped off by a local.)

My first stop, the Western Supermarket in Mountain Brook, a sub-urb of Birmingham, actually had a wine staff of three—and an impressive selection of California bottles. The Piggly Wiggly (yes, that is the name of a southern grocery store chain) had a charismatic young wine consultant named Andrew Brim who was particularly keen on Syrah.

I checked back recently to see if Mr. Brim was still with Piggy Wiggly. Yep, he was still on the floor selling wine. And he still loved Syrah, but it wasn't selling as well as Mr. Brim might have liked. And his store was still one of the best places in town to buy wine—not just because Mr. Brim had made some very good selections but because he knew what they tasted like as well.

Star Power

WHEN A PERSON BECOMES FAMOUS there are certain things that said famous person is expected to produce—or at least to promote. A sports stars needs a line of shoes—and preferably a clothing line, too. For A- and B-list celebrities, there should also be a perfume. Food is a bit trickier, and really no one can surpass the late Paul Newman in that category anyway; Paul Newman simply did food better than anyone else. Is there any celebrity salad dressing besides Paul Newman's you'd want on your greens or anyone else's pretzels you'd put in your travel bag?

And then of course there's wine, a product that's higher up the food chain than pretzels—and yet more commonplace. While there aren't many (any?) famous people who own pretzel factories, there are a lot of famous people who own vineyards: Sting, Dave Matthews, Nancy Pelosi, Danica Patrick, Tom Seaver, Francis Ford Coppola, and Angelina Jolie to name just a few.

And there are even more famous people willing to simply slap their name on a label, though oddly enough these wines tend to be made from the same grape. Why does every line of celebrity wines contain at least one Pinot Grigio? I don't understand it—at least not from a prestige standpoint. Why would a famous person want to put his or her name on a bottle of the world's most common, least-respected grape?

I know it's marketing, but why don't celebrities find some really obscure grape that he or she could call his or her own? How about a George Clooney Chenin Blanc? Or a Jennifer Lawrence Trousseau? (The Trousseau is the grape, by the way, not her wardrobe.) On second thought, Jennifer Lawrence might not be the best candidate for a celebrity wine label since she falls down at too many Important Awards Shows. She wouldn't want us thinking it was the fault of her Trousseau.

Why do celebrities choose to make—or pretend to make—wine anyway? There's the money, of course: famous people have lots of money and they have to find somewhere to spend it. (Very few will actually make money from wine.) As for putting their names on a cheap bottle of Pinot Grigio, I guess it's all about staying in the eye of the public, even if that public is seeing you when they're shopping in the grocery store wine aisle. (According to a Nielsen study I read, celebrity wine sales in grocery stores are strong. In 2007 celebrity wine sales rose almost 20 percent.)

But then as a commonplace person I only have conjecture and theory. But I vow that I will drink only wines by people who are famous because they made wine really, really well—and not just because they have an agent who got a great deal.

South Pole Chardonnay

WHAT KIND OF GRAPES WILL BE PLANTED by the next century's winemakers and where will they plant them? Will Champagne still be a suitable place to produce great sparkling wine, or will future growers turn to . . . Finland instead? Will Pinot Noir be pulled up in Burgundy and planted on the South Pole? However silly this sort of conjecture might sound, anything seems possible with the changing climate today.

In fact, the climatic changes have already begun. There is now Pinot Noir grown in far northern Germany where not so long ago there was none. There are even grapes grown in Great Britain and Ireland and Norway (one vineyard—so far).

While some wine regions have benefited from this warming trend (grapes are easier to get ripe), some have suffered, especially when greater warmth has led to drought. And when will it eventually be too warm to grow grapes at all? Scientists have predicted that famous wine regions such as Bordeaux and Burgundy may soon become too warm for their traditional grapes, Cabernet and Pinot Noir.

If that eventually happens, new grapes may have to be planted, something that no current-day Bordelais or Burgundian could probably countenance. How do you change out grapes that have been grown for centuries in the same place? And it's not just the vineyards that would have to change; the laws that dictate what grapes could be planted in which places would have to undergo a huge revision too.

Some places are expected to be less affected, such as high-elevation vineyards in places like Mendoza, Argentina. And some regions near bodies of water, particularly the ocean (like the Willamette Valley of Oregon), will fare better too. But growers in places like Western Australia have already had to deal with so much relentless heat they are very close to

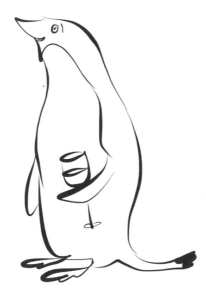

giving up on certain grapes like Cabernet. (Grapevines shut down when there's too much heat, and this means a loss of both color and acidity.)

Some places may disappear altogether, at least in winemaking terms. An international team of scientists predicted in 2013 that there will be massive changes to many of the most famous wine regions, including Napa and Tuscany. Some might even get as much as 70 or 80 percent smaller, thanks to the shift in climate, say these scientists. (They didn't say whether or not all the Napa millionaires would subsequently migrate to . . . Canada.)

And then of course there are other kinds of weather extremes, like the earthquake that hit Napa Valley in 2014, the frequent and devastating hailstorms in Burgundy, the damaging frost in New York's Finger Lakes. What will be the (long-term) impact of events such as these?

Finally, there will be—there has already been—a change in wine style as a result of climatic extremes. High-alcohol wines are likely to get even riper, with more alcohol, while cool-climate whites may get bigger and gain in alcohol too. Who knows how the wines of the next few decades will evolve? Perhaps the palates of wine drinkers will undergo a shift as radical as the climate change.

Drink-by Date

WHEN SHOULD I DRINK THIS? It's a question that you'll likely never hear a beer drinker pose. But it's something that a wine drinker might be obliged to ask if they've purchased a potentially "serious" wine—that is, a wine that should improve with time.

Some wineries will offer "drinking windows" of time on the back labels of bottles indicating when a wine will presumably be at its absolute peak. Of course, the labels of most great age-worthy wines (e.g., first-growth Bordeaux) will not offer this information; it's something you're expected to know or at least to find out for yourself.

This means consulting the wine merchant who sold you the wine or a wine critic. Both are in the business of offering advice on drinking times, presumably based on personal experience and an informed palate. Sometimes a wine critic might offer what seems like a very long period of time—as much as a decade or more. This means that the wine in question will hit a quality plateau and remain there for some time (though it could also mean the critic is hedging his or her bets).

A drinking window is really no more than an educated guess, based on a wine's past performance, taking into account variables like the growing conditions and the weather at harvest. For example, a wine that was produced in a hot year will develop differently than a wine from a rainy year or one made when everything was just right.

Although a drinking window should theoretically be based on a wine's track record, it isn't uncommon for wine critics to suggest drinking windows for wines that have only been produced for a vintage or two. This is likely based on certain generalizations about the wines of the region or the winemaker's style, but some might consider it the wine equivalent of a Hail Mary pass.

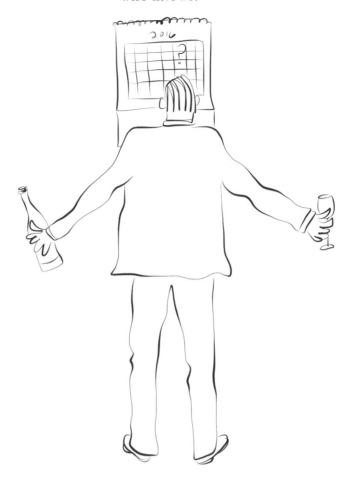

The best—if perhaps the most pricey—solution to the drinking window dilemma would be to buy a case of the wine in question and taste it, bottle by bottle, over a period of time to find when it peaks for your palate. Do you like a lot of juicy fruit, coupled to some possibly fierce tannins? You might want to drink it right away. Do you like soft tannins and more muted fruit? You might like the effect of ten years' aging time.

The good news about drinking windows for those who may be baffled by the concept is that they are almost entirely irrelevant. Very little wine (less than 5 percent, some pundits say) produced in the world improves with time. In fact, the drinking window for almost all the wine produced in the world is the same as the one for beer: right away.

Is Your Wine Bad or Just Dumb?

THERE IS A PERIOD OF TIME that some wines simply go "dumb." A dumb wine is a wine that has nothing to say—at least for a while. Dumb means a wine has "shut down" and it's not showing much in the way of fruit or aromas, although it's a more colorful if somewhat confusing way to say it.

I've had a few wines that I've been told were "dumb" and a few wines that I actually hoped were dumb and not simply characterless. Confusingly enough, characterless is how a dumb wine will taste. But a dumb wine can get "smart" again, while a characterless wine never will gain interest over time.

The notion of a dumb wine isn't fully understood, and wines can go dumb at any time. It's a phase that can last for several years—and there is no way of telling when—or if—the wine will reemerge. The only way you can definitively tell is if you've had the wine many times at several stages in its life; only then can you declare that it's not just characterless and dull but certifiably dumb.

Certain wines have reputations for playing dumb for a period of years—middle-aged Bordeaux, for example. A young Bordeaux may be open, which is to say fruity and accessible, in its youthful years, then shut down for an indeterminate period and then reemerge. And there are others. Some reds and whites from the northern Rhône go dumb, as does some red Burgundy, which is actually said by many wine collectors to open and close several times over the course of its life—another reason why Burgundy is one of the most frustrating wines in the world.

Some wine collectors think that a dumb/closed wine can be "opened" by aeration—that is, by decanting it and then waiting for a few hours—since the aroma is one of the aspects of a wine that is lost when it's shut down. Others don't believe this is true, that only time can reopen a wine.

One definitive way of telling a dumb wine from a bad one, according to one waggish wine drinker, is that a mediocre wine can be labeled "dumb" if it cost the drinker a great deal of money; otherwise, it's just a(nother) mediocre wine.

At First Sip

ALMOST EVERYONE I KNOW REMEMBERS THE TASTE of his or her first wine. Or his or her first memorable wine (they are sometimes but not always one and the same). In my case, the two wines were very different. My first wine was Boone's Farm Tickle Pink, a wine (or was it a "wine product"?) that sadly no longer exists. (It's noted on the Boone's Farm website that it's one of the many "retired flavors" along with some other has-beens like Blackberry Ridge.)

Tickle Pink was pink, it was sweet, and I'm sure it must have been fairly low alcohol, too. It was the perfect wine for a sixteen-year-old. But it didn't inspire me to want to drink more. In fact, I didn't drink much wine at all for another three years. And it was four more years before I had my first memorable bottle: a Wente Chardonnay.

I bought it from a department store in Columbus, Ohio, where they had a wine section. (The store sadly no longer exists.) I had researched the possibilities for several weeks and I made my selection quite carefully. Decades ago, Wente was one of the few prestigious California labels, although the Livermore-based winery is nearly forgotten today. I was unreasonably proud of my wine (which I seem to recall was pretty good but certainly not great). It was as if I did more than just buy it; I created an entire experience around it for my family, and I have the photo somewhere to prove that: five people gathered around a table staring reverentially at a bottle of Chardonnay. Or maybe that was just me.

My friends have all reported pretty similar experiences—a humble first wine (Manischewitz showed up quite often) followed by a memorable wine that was good but not necessarily great—like my bottle of

Wente Chardonnay. The memorable aspect was invariably the surrounding occasion. In my case, it was college graduation.

My friend Gabrielle's first wine was Blue Nun ("ghastly sweet," she says now in her grown-up state, though she probably loved it back in the day). But her first memorable wine was something else altogether. She was living in France with an "adopted" Burgundian family, and her French father gave her a glass of Montrachet. Gabrielle thought it was divine—at which point her French father told her that it was because Burgundy had such exceptional terroir, that their wines were better than those belonging to anyone else. She put it down to French chauvinism at the time, but over the years she says she has "come to see he was right."

It was the experience, the gift of the glass, that made the wine memorable—not just the greatness of the terroir. That's because wine has such an enormous emotional component, and the resonance of a particular bottle—especially early in one's drinking career—has almost everything to do with the context of its consumption. And while my friend Gabrielle was lucky to have that Montrachet, as true oenophiles know, it's the people and the place that make a wine truly resonate.

A Thaw in the North

I RECENTLY BOUGHT A VERY NICE CANADIAN RIESLING in a Brooklyn wine shop. I bought it in part because I rarely see Canadian wines for sale in this country but also because its sales card claimed it was made by "the best winemaker in Canada."

It was a big—if perhaps odd—sort of boast. It was as if the wine merchant considered Canada the equivalent of Michigan or New York (never mind it's the second largest country in the world). On the other hand, calling a winemaker the best in Michigan might also be a bit odd—if only because it's questionable how many wine drinkers (outside of Michigan) would actually think this was much of a credential.

Did the card attract much notice, many prospective drinkers? I asked the merchant, who seemed surprised by my question. "Not much," he admitted. Even a wine from the best winemaker in Canada wasn't enough to persuade skeptical wine drinkers in Brooklyn, I guess.

And yet wine has been made in Canada for hundreds of years, not only in Ontario but also in Quebec, Nova Scotia, and British Columbia (most famously in the Okanagan Valley). There are lots of fruit wines produced in other provinces too. But Canadian wine? I'll bet there are far fewer lovers of Canadian wine than there are of Canadian beer.

The only Canadian wine that has made much of an inroad in the United States over the years is Ice Wine, a dessert wine produced by grapes that are frozen on the vine. (The sugars in the wine don't freeze but the water does, yielding an intensely sweet wine.) In certain countries like Germany, where the practice originated, it might not be cold enough to produce Ice Wine every year. But in Canada, particularly in the Niagara Peninsula, it freezes quite reliably. And Inniskillin, made in the Niagara

Peninsula, is probably the one Canadian wine that regularly shows up on American wine shelves.

But there are many other sorts of wine made in Canada now. There are Chardonnays and Pinot Noirs and Syrahs and Merlots. The first two are particularly good in the Niagara Peninsula of Ontario, as are wines made from grapes like Riesling, Gamay, and Cabernet Franc. Nevertheless, very few Canadian wines are sold in the United States. One of the reasons may be a matter of distribution and taxes, but then the Canadians themselves haven't done much to further their cause—or, for that matter, their image. They don't export a lot of wine to the States but more distressingly they even created a category called International Canadian Blended.

An International Canadian Blended wine is one that can be produced with a significant percentage of non-Canadian grapes and yet still bear the name "Canada wine." The grapes could come from anywhere—South Africa, Argentina, or Washington State. The idea is to augment Canadian production with cheaper grapes.

There are sections of wine shops in Canada devoted to these ICB wines—and often times they are even larger than the sections devoted to "real" Canadian or VQA (Vintners Quality Alliance) wines. That's because the blended wines are much cheaper, I guess. It costs a lot more to grow Chardonnay grapes in Ontario than it does in, say, Chile.

This may be a boon for some Canadian producers who have had trouble getting a good crop when the weather is bad (see under: Ice Wine), but it doesn't convey a very confident message to potential Canadian wine drinkers. Do they really want a bottle that says, "Produced in Canada from Chilean grapes"? Our friends to the north deserve better representation.

Balancing Act

TEN OR EVEN TWENTY YEARS FROM NOW, wine drinkers may look back at this period in time as one in which everyone claimed to make or to drink—or just talked about—"balanced" wine.

The "B" word may be the most fashionable one in wine today. Sommeliers sell balanced wines, wine writers pen homages to balanced bottles, and there is even a group of "balanced" winemakers with a society of their own. What their moniker, In Pursuit of Balance (IPOB), lacks in musicality it makes up for in purposefulness.

The IPOBers (California producers of Pinot Noir and Chardonnay who are mostly young and good looking) define a wine that is "balanced" as one that is non-manipulated and non-enhanced in any way. That means, for example, no addition of acid or sugar and no adjustment of alcohol in any way (there are devices that will do this, and many winemakers employ them). They want to create wines that are as "authentic" as possible, they say. *Authentic* is another favorite word of these balanced folk.

A balanced wine is one that isn't high in alcohol, so say the Pursuiters (my nickname, not theirs). One of the founders of the club even has a number that the wines he considers balanced cannot exceed (14.2 percent alcohol). If this seems a touch arbitrary, it is—much in the same way that the difference between a horse and a pony is determined in part by their respective heights. (In an eerie coincidence it's actually the same number: 14.2 hands.)

There is a Manifesto of Balance that outlines all the various requirements that a balanced wine is expected to meet; there is probably a Balanced Handshake as well. It's all very clubby and certainly exclusionary—and also it seems to suggest that anyone producing Chardonnay or Pinot Noir who is not in their group may be, well, just a little unbalanced.

Balance is a subjective and objective word. It applies to both perception and fact. If a wine is excessively oaky, for example, the oak will stand out. Ditto a wine with lots of alcohol. An imbalance will reveal itself. Or at least that's the usual idea of a balanced wine. All the components of the wine should be in harmony: the fruit, the alcohol, and the oak. But then each wine drinker has a different tolerance of each of these elements; some might tolerate, even prefer, a bit of oak, a bit more fruit. One person's imbalanced wine is another person's delight. Who gets to be the Goldilocks of wine who decides when something is "just right"?

Balance is most certainly something worth pursuing, but I'm pretty sure it's ever fleeting—in wine as in life.

Glad Handing

WHAT IS IT ABOUT HANDS AND WINE? Wines are made by hand. They are harvested by hand. They are crafted by hands-on winemakers. When a hand is involved with a wine these days, it's inevitably a well-publicized one. But why, in this age of advanced technology, are hands the most-touted instruments today?

One would guess it's a shorthand (!) way of expressing a wine's authenticity. A wine that a hand has helped to form is a wine that is personal and somehow more "real." It's a wine with a source—the place or the person who created it.

The power of the hand can also be seen in the number of wineries with *hand* in their name. The Two Hands winery in the Barossa Valley of Australia is one of the region's most distinctive properties, where all the wines are—naturally—"made by hand" by producer Michael Twelftree and presumably his team. There is 14 Hands wines in Washington State, which is actually named for the wild mustangs not for seven people who are working at the estate. (A hand, in this case, is a reference to a measurement of a horse; a small horse, like the mustang, is often no more than 14 hands high.)

There is Hearts & Hands winery in New York's Finger Lakes, which may win the top prize for a double-whammy of emotion, Black Hand Cellars in California, and Sleight of Hand Cellars in Washington State, whose name suggests that a magician has done some work in the winery—though it might also suggest something a bit unsettling as to the wines' authenticity.

My favorite, however, in terms of sheer seeming-chutzpah is the Hand of God winery in Mendoza, Argentina. Actually, the name is meant to be a reference to a famous goal scored by an Argentine soccer player and not the vinous intervention of a deity. The wines at Hand of God are hand-harvested and the grapes hand-sorted, although the winery doesn't note exactly whose hand was actually involved in those acts.

And yet, despite all this hand-championing, there have been crucial advances in winemaking technology in recent years that do not involve hands. There are machines that harvest grapes in the gentlest of ways, fermentation tanks that allow winemakers to program (with their hands!) the exact time and temperature conditions under which they want their wines to ferment. There are machines to extract alcohol and machines that can add water back. While some of these have helped to make some pretty industrial and unpalatable stuff, some have also made wine much better than it might otherwise have been or kept a winery from going bankrupt!

Although there are some wine drinkers who would like to believe that no good can come of technology, I see it a bit differently. Any winemaker whose goal is a wine with personality and character is someone who deserves—yes—a hand.

Price and Perception

SOMETIMES PEOPLE ASK ME QUESTIONS about wine whose answers seem obvious. One that is posed pretty often has to do with comparative costs. What is the difference between a ten-dollar wine and a hundred-dollar wine? (The exact numbers vary, of course.)

While the obvious answer is ninety dollars, I resist the temptation of a glib retort and give one of two answers. The first is the simplest: some wines simply cost more than others to produce. They may be made in small amounts; they require the use of expensive new oak or are made from grapes purchased from a famous vineyard. They might also be in great demand, and that alone can drive up the price.

The second answer is perception. While the spread between a ten-dollar and a hundred-dollar bottle is too big for the difference to be with the sales and marketing alone, the position of a wine in the market is a big part of the pricing equation. I've had several (off-the-record) conversations with winemakers in Napa who have fretted that their price was too cheap compared with the producers they considered peers. (Yes, there are actually winemakers who think that in the Napa Valley.) They worry that their wine will seem like it's not the equal of its peers if it's priced twenty-five or thirty dollars less a bottle.

Never mind whether or not that is fair—or if there is already a sufficient profit built in; winery owners don't like the perception that their wine isn't one of the best. And price, for some people, is the only information that they have if they don't know anything else about the wine, the winery, or the region. They can at least say, "I paid a hundred dollars for this." (And we all know wine drinkers who like to say that.)

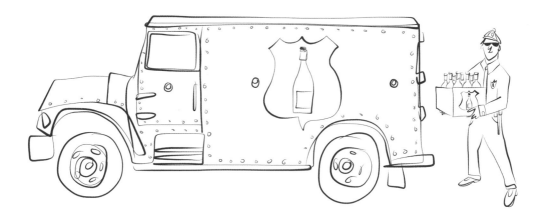

But back to the very first question. In most cases, I would respond with my own question: Why do you ask? If someone wants to know whether or not a ten-dollar wine is just as good as one that costs ten times as much, they are probably seeking validation of their own taste more than the truth. They want to know—or to believe—that they don't need to spend a great deal of money to get a wine that's just as good—or almost as good as—something expensive.

And there have been studies made (many times) that show people could only tell the expensive wine from the cheap about half the time—about the same amount of times as random chance. Perhaps it's just a matter of switching the price tags?

The Nose Knows

ALTHOUGH JUST ABOUT EVERYONE TALKS ABOUT WINE in terms of how it tastes rather than how it smells, this is rarely an accurate reference. The "taste" of a wine is almost always the way it smells. It has been said that some 80 percent of a wine's character can be found in its aromas alone. In short, what matters most is your nose.

The late, great Bordeaux oenologist Émile Peynaud wrote in his definitive work, *The Taste of Wine*, that the sense of smell "appears to be ten thousand times more sensitive than that of taste." The nose is the most powerful instrument a wine lover can possess, and with careful training a practiced wine taster (wine smeller?) can detect hundreds of different substances. (Perfumers have this ability too.) The tongue, on the other hand, gets only a few: salty, sweet, bitter, sour, and unami.

The fruit notes that most wine drinkers find in their glass—cherry, strawberry, raspberry, et al.—are all notes that are found by the nose. Ditto the wood, the spicy, the vegetal, and the wide range of flowers, too—they're all aromas, not flavors.

These aromas are best appreciated by what's called "retronasal breathing," which literally means "breathing through your nose" (with your mouth closed) and is accomplished by taking a sip of wine, swirling it around the surface of your tongue while inhaling deeply and then exhaling. This will bring the aromas of the wine more fully into your nasal passages (and it's not nearly as complicated as it sounds).

But odors are evanescent and rapidly dissipate, so when one is smelling a wine it's best to stick your nose in a glass briefly but often—short, hard sniffs of only a few seconds each. Since odors aren't persistent (meaning they don't stay long in the air) then a long, sustained smell won't yield a more sustained smell.

And yet, no matter how well we train our noses to detect aromas and match them with certain types of wine or certain places, we're ultimately no match for an animal. Professor Peynaud further notes that our sense of smell, no matter how acute, is no match for many mammals or even insects for whom a sense of smell is primary. In *The Taste of Wine*, the professor wrote, "According to one ethnological hypothesis, when man began to walk upright some of his ability to smell was lost in favor of the senses of sight and hearing."

In other words, we can't actually smell a wine as well as a dog or a cat or even a possum, but at least we're much better at holding a glass.

Ode to the Obscure

MEMORIZE A LOT OF OBSCURE INFORMATION and you're sure to be taken (mistaken) for someone who knows a lot. This rule applies to all sorts of things, from world history to politics to theater to, especially, wine. Those who possess the greatest amount of the most obscure information (read: restaurant sommeliers) command the greatest respect, not to mention power, over everyone else.

Or at least that's how wine drinkers who can't find Styria on a map (it's in Austria) or describe the taste of the Favorita grape (high acidity) might feel. But the most important reason to have a good grasp of the obscure is that the knowledge can help you get a good wine at a very good price.

The familiar always costs more than the obscure—that's not just a rule of thumb but a near certainty. It's the reason why a Napa Cabernet or a Sancerre will never be a good deal. Those wines have such a built-in constituency they sell themselves. (A prominent wine director in New York once told me that he could price Sancerre at just about any amount and it would sell.)

But a bottle of Quincy? That's something else altogether. Few wine drinkers know that it's also a wine made from Sauvignon Blanc just a few miles down the road from Sancerre. And yet armed with this information, a wine drinker who is daring and/or short of funds can have a wine like Sancerre for less than half the price.

And there's more. In fact, there's an obscure alternative to practically every famous example. Love Barolo, the noble wine of Piedmont, but don't have the coin for the best names? Try Gattinara or Ghemme—they're both made from Nebbiolo (the same grape as Barolo), taste almost alike, and the better examples can age nearly as long.

Need another example? How about the wines of Saint-Aubin for white Burgundy lovers who don't want to pay in the low three figures for Chassagne or Puligny? Producers like Hubert Lamy and Pierre Yves Colin are making beautiful examples of wines from this appellation, which borders both the Chassagne and Puligny appellations and offers white wines with the same kind of bright acidity and crystalline minerality at a fraction of the price of its neighbors.

These wines can be found in the same section of a wine list as their more famous brethren or in that catch-all category called "Miscellaneous" (which is sometimes simply called "Other" or more promisingly "Interesting Finds").

If it's the latter, it's probably more likely the sommelier actually likes the wines (a category called "Other" suggests that he or she may have been bullied into buying it by a fast-talking wine salesperson). But a wine that the sommelier deems an "interesting find" is one that the sommelier probably loves as well and couldn't resist buying even if it didn't have a logical place on the list. An obscure wine requires the sommelier to engage and excite a would-be drinker—transforming a commodity into a cause.

It's well worth developing your own list of obscure wines. It will not only broaden your mind and your palate, it will almost certainly save you lots of money as well.

A Country in Transition

I'VE NEVER BEEN TO SOUTH AFRICA. But every oenophile I know who has visited that country talks first in terms of its tremendous visual beauty. They speak of its stunning views, of its oceans and valleys and its rugged mountains. Eventually they get around to talking about the wines. Much better than expected, they'll say. Some wines were actually very good. And then they'll go right back to talking about the land, sea, and sky.

These sort of travelogues have made me long to visit South Africa, but, alas, most of the South African wines that I've tasted over the years haven't made me long for more South African wines.

Wine has been made in South Africa for hundreds of years (starting in the seventeenth century), and once upon a time the wines from Constantia were considered some of the best in the world. But there have been many ups and downs in South African winemaking since those days. The longest down probably came during the Apartheid years when almost no wines were exported from the country and a cooperative known as KWV kept tight control of the domestic market. It promoted quantity over quality and emphasized fortified over table wine. I recall that the wine shop in New York where I worked during the Apartheid era carried KWV wines but kept them hidden away. Only South Africans—and the KWV customers were always South African—would know to ask for them by name.

One of the best South African wines, then and now, goes by the rather inelegant name of Steen. Taken from the Dutch word for "stone," it was the most important, most planted white grape in the country for a very long time (and still is today). But it was only fairly recently that

South Africans found out that their Steen was in fact Chenin Blanc. That's what it's now called on most South African wine labels, although a few die-hards still favor *Steen*. There are some terrific old vine Chenin/Steens in South Africa, but, sadly, there's not a huge export market for it so many winemakers are ripping it out.

The South African Syrahs, aka Shirazes, seem to be more marketable—and Syrah is an up-and-coming variety for many winemakers there, who also seem to like the fact that its big flavors (spice, black pepper, blackberry) match well with their national dish (braai). Merlot is another red that's fairly well represented in South Africa. Cabernet Sauvignon is king in South Africa (as it is everywhere else in the world), and it grows well in key wine subregions like Swartland, Durbanville and Stellenbosch.

The one grape grown in South Africa I will never understand is Pinotage. It's the country's star grape, for better or worse. (It's the latter, for sure, as far as I'm concerned.) I've never loathed a grape the way I loathe Pinotage. It was created in 1925 by a professor of viticulture at Stellenbosch University who crossed Pinot Noir with Cinsaut—with the idea it would possess the virtues of each grape: the elegance and aromas of Pinot Noir, the hardiness of Cinsaut. Instead, he created a wine with aromas of nail polish, burned tire, and old animal pelt. It's a wine that you have to hold your nose to drink.

I've tried to find reasons to love Pinotage—or at least to accept it—over the years. I staged a big Pinotage tasting a few years ago and found a few wines that really weren't bad. I even found one I liked a great deal (Beyerskloof Diesel—named after the winery dog). But I also provoked the wrath of some loyal South Africans, who took great umbrage at the idea that I didn't much like Pinotage to begin with. They sent angry emails and posted comments on blogs. It was as if I had burned their national flag, not simply scorned their flagship grape. Perhaps I will have to delay my trip to South Africa until a time when the Pinotage has all been ripped up and replaced with Syrah.

In Praise of Mediocrity

DO YOU EVER WANT to drink a wine that is merely okay? That doesn't stir your soul or make you do cartwheels but that simply quenches your thirst?

In the serious world of wine where I (mostly) reside, I realize this is fairly blasphemous talk—and yet it's crossed my mind more than once. I'm so used to looking at wine critically and looking for complexities and challenges and, yes, flaws that sometimes the simple pleasure of drinking wine can be lost. A simple wine is a wine of one rather than multiple notes. And maybe that's not always so bad.

Several years ago I was in Paris visiting my friend and her husband, who I didn't know very well. The three of us went to a bistro for lunch. We each ordered a glass of the house rosé—a Bordeaux. It wasn't anything special—in fact it was quite mediocre. I commented briefly on this fact and briefly enumerated its shortcomings.

My friend's husband was annoyed. "Why can't you just enjoy the wine?" he asked. "Why do you have to analyze everything?" What he meant was, Why can't you enjoy this moment? Spring in Paris? This bistro meal? And perhaps he also meant, and didn't say, How do you know I wasn't enjoying this crummy rosé?

At the time I felt a bit defensive—it was my job, after all, to pay attention to wine, to catalog its virtues and its mistakes. It was only much later that I realized that my friend's husband might have had a point. Wine doesn't always have to deliver complexity or an intellectual challenge. It doesn't need to be a focal point. Sometimes it can just be an adjunct to a meal. It's even all right for it to be something (much) less than great.

A Gift of Wine

WINE IS ONE OF THE EASIEST GIFTS for someone to give and to receive. Even the gift of the wrong bottle can be easily rectified by bestowing it upon another—who may, in turn, do the same with a wine of his or her own. Indeed, I've been given bottles that I'm sure have passed through more than a few hands before landing in mine—at least until I regifted them too. (I've found that tawny Port is a particular favorite among serial regifters.)

Of course, some wines will be more gratefully received than others, but if you follow my five rules of wine gift giving you'll please most of the recipients (almost) all of the time and reduce the number of times your bottle will be regifted as well.

Give a magnum

A magnum of wine is equal to two bottles, but the sum, especially visually, is much greater than its parts. A magnum looks like a lot—like four or five bottles instead of two. (This is a magical magnum fact.) A magnum exudes magnanimousness and plentitude—and perhaps the even more cheerful message that the giver is careless with cash. The wine inside is almost irrelevant because the bottle size is so perfect. Note: the one exception to this rule is a magnum purchased in a supermarket. That will have exactly the opposite effect.

Better red than white

I don't believe that red wine is inherently superior to white—and I drink equal amounts of both colors. But for some reason most people seem to

believe red is the more sophisticated drink—it's what you "graduate" to after training time with white. And because this particular piece of misinformation is (still) bandied about, if I had to choose between the two colors for a gift, I'd always go with red.

Avoid the obscure

I once brought a bottle of very good Moscato d'Asti to a very wealthy man's house. He had no idea what it was except that it was a Sparkling Wine That Was Not Champagne. He left it on the sideboard near the front door (no doubt hoping that someone—perhaps his housekeeper?—would take it away). He didn't thank me for the bottle and clearly didn't consider it a present—it was just too odd and too far outside his experience. A lesson learned: don't give a wine that's too obscure.

Sparkling is best

Although red wine is safer than white, Champagne is the safest of all. Preferably not a brand name that's available everywhere (so the host knows how much you spent) but one that's cleverly packaged—preferably with lots of gold type. I'd suggest looking for Champagnes from a little-known producer as opposed to a big name like Moët & Chandon, although I might be in danger of violating rule number three by this suggestion.

Resist the gift set

No wine that is worth drinking ever requires anything extra. If wine glasses or a picnic basket or even a corkscrew are added to enhance the package, you can be fairly certain the producer of the wine is hoping that you'll overlook what's actually inside the bottle. And anything that comes wrapped in cellophane should also be avoided. Unless, of course, it's an actual bottle of Cristal—in which case the recipient is a very good friend, your accountant, or a rock star.

A Certain Reserve

"I ALWAYS BUY A RESERVE WINE," my uncle once said to me in a tone that suggested he was imparting a great piece of advice. "The reserve wine is always the best," my uncle added, in case I had missed the point.

My uncle is a very smart man who built a very successful business and he made some very good money, but he is what you might call a naïf when it comes to wine. He's exactly the audience that wineries have in mind when they create those "Reserve" wines—the wines that have nothing more than marketing and fancy labels to distinguish them from the "non-reserve" stuff.

There is no accepted definition or legal mandate for the meaning of "reserve" in many winemaking regions of the world. There are exceptions, of course. There are regions in Spain (Rioja) and Italy (Tuscany) where the wine must undergo additional aging to be called "reserve," but there are far more places where it is no more than a matter of a fancy—and often expensive—word where there is no legal minimum aging or exclusivity of site.

Under ideal circumstances a reserve wine is a loftier expression of the "regular" bottling—perhaps because the vineyard site is exceptional or the clonal selection is rare, or the harvest was exceptional. Or all of the above.

"Reserve" is like "old vine"—another phrase that has no legal meaning. An old vine can be ten years old or twenty years or a hundred years old. Only the winemaker has to decide what qualifies as old. Then he or she can call it "old" and rest assured almost no one will ask, "Old relative to what?"

Both phrases are almost a guarantee that the price will go up. And if it's a reserve wine made from old vines, well, all bets are off. By the way, this does seem more commonplace with American wines than those from Europe—perhaps because Europeans have more stringent rules about what constitutes a reserve wine—or because they have a lot of vines that are legitimately old.

I did mention my misgivings about this to my uncle, by the way. He was dismayed to learn he'd been taken in by some clever marketing all these years. He asked what he should do. I suggested he undertake a (blind) test. Why not buy the "regular" wine and the "reserve" and find out if he could discern the difference? Maybe he would find that he still liked the reserve or perhaps he'd find that the regular wine was actually better or at least just as good. My uncle said he'd try it and let me know how it worked.

A few months later, my uncle called sounding jubilant. He wasn't buying any more reserve wines, he said. He'd seen the light. He didn't become a success in the world by being taken in by a bunch of words. And, by the way, he was saving money, as well.

Thank You for Spitting

ONE OF THE MOST CRITICAL COMPONENTS of wine tasting does not involve drinking but spitting. A lot of spitting, over and over again. In fact, no wine professional worth his or her weight in Chardonnay is less than adept at this crucial act. Spitting is the difference between remembering the names and the profiles of the twenty or thirty wines that you've tasted and forgetting them all (and possibly embarrassing yourself).

But an effective spitting technique isn't easily acquired—it can take years to perfect just the right form—the ideal liquid arc—which is quite important if you are tasting in a crowded room of wine professionals or even just spitting into a cup at home.

There are informal categories of spitters that reveal the taster's relative prowess or lack of it. There's the drinker, the person who somehow can't manage to bring him or herself to actually spit the wine out. I have friends who fit into this category. One says he can't do it in sheer physical terms. Another said she feels too self-conscious to pull it off. And yet a third claims he doesn't want to "waste" the wine.

There are tasters who try—but don't completely succeed. These are the dribblers, the ones who can't seem to get all of the wine all the way out of their mouths. It gets caught somewhere on the way down. This comes from lack of practice and taking too large a mouthful of wine.

For anyone just learning to spit, it might be best to start with something nonalcoholic—water is good. It might also be a good idea not to take too large a mouthful. And don't try to aim terribly far. The shorter the distance, the better things will go for a spitting tyro. The more you practice, the more distance you can acquire: the late Alexis Bespaloff, a great wine writer and an even greater wine spitter, was called the "Baryshnikov of the bucket" for the accuracy of his aim and the impressive rainbow-style arc of his wine.

The good news is that most spitting receptacles in professional settings are fairly large—they're usually ice buckets or large spittoons—and there is no shame in bringing it up to your face to make sure you get it all inside the bucket. Sometimes wineries will even allow—or encourage—tasters to spit on the floor. Mind you, this is only the case if the floor is dirt or you are spitting into a drain on the floor (which is generally rather difficult, so beginners would do well to request a bucket).

The worst part about spitting? It's not the "waste" of the wine—or red wine on your shoes—but the occasional overfilled bucket. This can result in one of the least pleasant parts of wine tasting: the backsplash. This condition occurs when there is simply too much wine spit in the bucket and yours causes an overflow—which flows back on the spitter. I've seen some pretty ugly backsplash incidents, though none uglier than when a well-known wine writer wearing a white suit (points for bravery!) got covered in a backsplash bath of red wine.

That brings me to my last and perhaps most important point about spitting: whenever possible, wear black.

Mass Delirium

IF THERE IS A SPECIAL OCCASION—an art gallery opening, the publication of a book, or even a marriage—one thing is almost certain: the wine will be bad. I don't know why this is a near-inviolate rule but, as one who has attended plenty of weddings, book parties, and art openings over many years and consumed (or pretended to consume) my share of bad wine, I can attest that this is just about always true.

It doesn't matter if the artwork in question costs millions of dollars or the book is a best seller or the betrothed pair had no problem spending $100,000 on flowers, the wine will be an alcoholic afterthought, often sourced from Chile or even Brazil

I've offered to lend assistance, especially when it's a bride or groom I know and I'll (also) be drinking the stuff. A few brides (it's always the brides, for some reason) have taken me up on my offer, but never as often as you might think—or that I might hope.

I'm guessing that there are several reasons why this is the case—though mind you I don't regard any of them as particularly good. The first one is money. Few people seem willing to spend more than a few bucks on something that is to be quickly consumed. That's the only rationale I can ascribe to the choice of Brazilian Merlot. (Yes, I actually drank this at a friend's wedding and, no, I will not name names.) I'd like to know what they spent on flowers. I guarantee they cost more than the wine.

The second reason is actually a close cousin to the first or perhaps a rationalization: no one will care. The idea is that everyone will be swept away by the art or the book or the beauty of the wedding and not notice that they're drinking swill. While this may be true of really amazing artwork or a particularly astonishing work of fiction, I am convinced there is no marital union so joyful that it can't be dampened by a Brazilian Merlot.

Right of First Refusal

ONE OF THE MOST POTENTIALLY FRAUGHT MOMENTS while dining out occurs early in the meal, when the waiter or sommelier opens the wine bottle. You've been shown the bottle, you've examined the label, and now you are obliged to give it a taste. (You might also be handed the cork, but don't smell it. It's just further proof that this is the actual bottle you ordered. The name of the wine or the winery will be on the cork.)

Tasting the wine at this point is not to ascertain whether or not you like it (although hopefully you will) but to determine whether or not it is flawed. Is it corked? That's a wine tainted with a compound called TCA that commonly affects corks and makes the wine smell like wet newspapers or worse. Is it perhaps oxidized? That's what happens when air seeps in and spoils the wine. An oxidized wine looks and smells a bit like Sherry—the same dark gold in color and the same yeasty smell.

What if the wine isn't corked or oxidized but it just doesn't taste right? There are a lot of reasons why this may be true—including the fact that it may just be an unfamiliar wine or an odd grape. (Hopefully the sommelier will warn you about these sorts of wines—or put asterisks and notes next to them on the wine list.)

But should you find anything unpleasant in your glass you will be forced to utter those most dreaded words (the ones you dread saying and that your waiter dreads hearing even more): "I need to send this wine back."

Many restaurants will do just about anything they can to avoid the use of this phrase—often by having a sommelier taste each bottle before it is poured. This is a fairly pain-free solution, except that some people resent it, believing the sommelier just wants to drink some of their wine. (Occasionally this might be the case but not very often.)

If a sommelier isn't around to taste or observe, you will have to decide if the wine is sound all on your own. And it's a pressure-filled few moments. Everyone is waiting and staring—and thirsty, of course. And you've got to render a potentially expensive bit of judgment in a few seconds or less.

Hopefully you will find that the wine is good and it can be poured. But one last word: some flaws aren't readily apparent. Sometimes they take time—several minutes or more—to show. I've had mildly corked wines that didn't taste or smell overtly bad but grew worse over time. That's what a corked wine will often do. But how do you send back a half-finished bottle?

The answer: you don't. You could try to explain to the sommelier (or waiter) that the wine changed in your glass. You could ask to order a different wine and hope you won't be charged for the first (unlikely). Or you can do what most people do in this situation—simply drink it—and take comfort knowing that a bad wine won't hurt you. It just isn't very much fun.

The Chardonnay Conundrum

WHAT IS IT ABOUT CHARDONNAY that inspires so much enmity among wine drinkers? Is there another grape in the world whose name has been invoked with greater disdain or actually occasioned the formation of a grape haters' club?

I'm referring to ABC, or the Anything but Chardonnay group. This informal movement of (mostly) wine professionals decided back in the 1990s that a backlash against the grape was due and they began to campaign against Chardonnay—and champion in its place the wines that they considered more "pure," like Riesling or Chenin Blanc. They derided all Chardonnays, saying they tasted and smelled like lemon and cream or popcorn or butterscotch.

This wasn't true of all Chardonnays, of course, and there are plenty of other wines that taste and smell worse. Maybe it was because Chardonnay was such a popular wine that they resented the fact that people liked it so much.

The ABC-ers didn't accomplish very much if you consider that Chardonnay is still the number one white grape among American wine drinkers and that just about every wine producer in this country and others turns out a version of the grape.

That's because the Chardonnay grape can be just about anything that a winemaker envisions. Chardonnay may be the World's Most Malleable Grape. Which means that while it can smell like buttered popcorn if a winemaker wishes it so, it can also be wonderfully bright and pure, as with Chablis. The latter is a Chardonnay that possesses the sort of brilliant transparency accorded to Riesling (which is a favorite grape of the ABC club).

Of course, Chardonnay is also quite friendly with oak. Whether French or American or Slavonian or Hungarian, Chardonnay and oak go together like a hand in a glove, although sometimes the glove is velvet and sometimes the glove is more like steel. It's overt or subtle, depending on what the winemaker wants it to be.

There are plenty of people who like oak—or at least the flavors that it imparts, spice or tropical notes. Some don't care for this at all—and inveigh against "oaky Chardonnay." I've met wine drinkers who actually assume that all Chardonnay is oaked—as if it were some sort of intrinsic component of the grape itself.

Chardonnay will never go away—it's just too useful and too beloved by too many others. It probably won't ever be any less popular than it is today—not just among wine drinkers but winemakers as well. It works so well in so many places, from Burgundy to Sonoma and various parts of northern Italy, to say nothing of Oregon and Washington State, that there's no way winemakers will be giving it up anytime soon. And it's particularly extraordinary when it's part of Champagne. That's what the anti-Chardonnay crowd overlooks: without Chardonnay, some of the best wines in the world would no longer exist.

In Good Company

WINE IS A BEVERAGE MEANT TO BE ENJOYED WITH OTHERS. Wine should always be accompanied by food. Wine should never be served too cold or too warm. These are just a few of the so-called rules of wine drinking that most oenophiles believe should be followed, though none may be more rigorously observed than rule number one: wine should never be consumed alone.

It's the one rule that I hear invoked over and over again—especially by many of the women I know. "I would never open a bottle of wine if I were at home by myself," a friend once confided to me, in a horrified tone. To her, a solo glass or two of a cheap Pinot Grigio was the first rocky step on the road to wrack if not ruin.

Another female friend, who's fairly frugal, said she would never open a bottle of wine on her own because there might be wine left over that she might never consume. Who knew when or how she might finish the bottle? What if she went out to dinner the following night—or wanted to drink something else instead? There were so many variables and, in any case, she would have easily wasted half a bottle or more, she said.

Most men I know seem to view solo drinking a bit differently. One friend cited the actual opening of a bottle as the reason why he would shy away from drinking wine alone. The simple act of pulling a cork out of the bottle somehow felt too showy, too ceremonial an act, according to my non-showy friend. (I had no idea opening wine was so dramatic for him.) And yet this friend had no problem opening a can of beer and drinking it alone—apparently there's less drama in the act of pulling a tab than a cork.

Another friend has so many really good wines in his cellar that he feels like they're being wasted if he drinks one of them all by himself. This was a slightly different take on my frugal friend's feeling except it was in some ways even sadder—it was as if he considered himself unworthy of his own wine.

The obvious answer—to me—is to drink wine in the company of others in a public setting like a restaurant or a bar. You're by yourself but you're not alone. The last time I ate dinner alone I ordered an entire bottle of wine (in part because I hate wines by the glass and in part because it was one of the most interesting wines on the list.) But I didn't drink the bottle myself; I shared it with the man next to me, who turned out to be the restaurant's chef who wanted a nice glass of wine too.

Wine is such a sociable beverage—and sharing it can solve someone else's dilemma along with your own.

Wine's Best Friend

WINE AND DOGS MAY NOT SEEM TO GO TOGETHER as readily as, say, cheese and wine, but it's a pairing that's just as strong and just as longstanding. After all, it's the rare winery that doesn't have a dog or two milling around the tasting room or roaming through the vineyard. Dogs and wine just seem to go together.

And a small publishing empire has been built by those who understood this particular bond. I've found a rather large collection of wine-dog books created in recent years—some devoted to wine dogs of the entire country, others to wine dogs of specific parts of the country like Napa, Washington State, Sonoma, and central California. There are even "deluxe editions" of these books for especially discerning dog-wine lovers (or is it wine-dog lovers?) or readers who don't want some ordinary combination of the two.

Full confession: I have a few of these books myself. And I like what I find, even if the prose isn't exactly Proustian. For example, according to my copy of *Wine Dogs USA* (volume 3, in fact), "wherever good wine is made, you're likely to find a dog scouting the tasting room or winery." I've found this to be a near-universal truth.

Perhaps wine critics think this way too, since Robert M. Parker, Jr., wrote the foreword in this series of books—in the "voice" of his bulldog Buddy Parker (whose portrait is featured as well, along with another Parker-owned pet, Betty Jane). Who wouldn't trust the ratings of a man who can channel the spirit of a bulldog?

And if a man or woman can or should be measured by his or her type of dog, I suppose it's not too much to measure the quality of a wine by the winery dog. Maybe it's even informational, too. If the winery dog is a German Shepherd you would expect a different style of wine than if the winery dog were, say, a Pekingese, wouldn't you?

It's a connection that might be worth exploring. In fact, I could probably find quite a few parallels. There's one book that I was given lately, however, that has me stumped: *Wine Cats*. The only wine that I can connect—and rather unfavorably—with a feline is Sauvignon Blanc. After all, it's a grape whose signature aromatic note is most commonly described as "cat pee."

It's a Fad, Fad World

A FADDISH WINE IS A WINE MARKETER'S DREAM and winemaker's nightmare. The reason for the former is clear. What's easier to sell than something that everyone has already demonstrated they want? At the same time, every winemaker knows there is a definite downside to a fad wine. When a particular wine—or type of wine—becomes wildly sought-after, it can be almost impossible to keep up with demand. And the demand is always Right Now, not three or four years down the road.

And that is, unfortunately, how grape growing works. It takes three or more likely four years for a new vine to bear good-quality fruit. And by that time the Pinot Noir/Syrah/Merlot or Chardonnay faddish drinkers may well have moved on.

As of this writing, Moscato is the biggest fad wine in the world thanks to a perfect storm of circumstance that included a growing taste for sweet wines among younger drinkers and its starring appearance in some popular rap songs. (When Drake sang about lobster and Moscato, he inspired a whole new audience of drinkers, many of whom found the song on YouTube, to visit wine stores.)

Some fads begin and never really end. Take, for example, the fad for Pinot Noir. Its faddishness is thought to have begun when the movie *Sideways* debuted. The loutish hero lionized Pinot and demonized Merlot. Everyone was calling it "the *Sideways* Effect"—though wine drinkers had already begun to pay more attention to Pinot Noir anyway. But right now it seems like their fascination with the grape is without end. Pinot Noir may be so enduringly popular it's no longer just a fad.

Of course, Syrah producers thought the same thing about their grape some fifteen or twenty years ago—when they planted lots of Syrah but ran out of places to sell it before they ran out of wine. The Syrah fad came and went so suddenly that by the time the grapes were mature, there was almost no demand for the wine.

And, of course, there have been fads not just for wines made from particular grapes but for brands. The names of these brands are like snapshots in history. There was the Yellow Tail era of the late 1990s, the wine coolers of Bartles & Jaymes of the '80s, predated of course by Blue Nun, Mateus, and, of course, Riunite—whose ad campaign convinced American wine drinkers what they really, really wanted was something sweet and red with a bit of fizz.

But fads are more fragmented today, in part because there are so many more wines—and brands—in play. And the communication is much more diverse as well. A wine doesn't need a television campaign or even a print ad in a paper—it can even become a hit thanks to a song played on YouTube. What about that Moscato and lobster?

Wine Legacies

WINE MAY BE the only agricultural product that can make even the toughest billionaire turn wistful. A winery, a vineyard, or a brand is a compelling kind of legacy that many a wealthy individual would like to be able to one day bequeath to a son or a daughter or a grandchild.

I've spent years talking with men and women—but mostly men— who have made fortunes in various businesses and much later decided to build or to buy their own winery. (The fortune is, of course, necessary before this can occur). I'm not sure why they do this; it rarely makes fiscal sense. But then dreams are as various as the people who dream them. I think it has something to do with the fact that wine is not just an agricultural product but an enduring symbol of a civilized life.

And of course there's a bit of ego, too. There aren't many places or products where you can create your own history and put your aesthetic sense on display for the world to see. And to buy.

That's a part of the equation that many aspiring winery owners often overlook: to have a legacy they have to sell the stuff. It's not just something for the next generation to inherit; it's a business that must be built—and cultivated—day in and day out.

Does it make any business sense? How much does a winery actually make? That's something that I've found some winery owners don't know and many more would not like to discuss—and definitely not with their peers. But according to a State of the Wine Industry Annual Report produced in 2013, the profits on a winery in 2012 were actually quite small. The estimate of annual pretax profit that year was a measly 6.9 percent, according to the annual Silicon Valley Bank report. And it might prove even smaller, since the price of land and grapes have all gone up.

That means that most would-be bequeathers are more likely to pass down some rather large debts. Perhaps all those legacy seekers who want their children or grandchildren to remember them fondly might consider investing in liquor, instead. Liquor is a lot easier to produce and has historically enjoyed larger profit margins than wine. It may be less romantic and it's definitely less scenic (how many families want to gather the generations around the gin still?), but at least there might be more money around for them to spend.

Nothing to See

GREAT MOVIES ABOUT FOOD ARE EASY TO NAME (*Like Water for Chocolate, Babette's Feast, Big Night, Eat Drink Man Woman*), but great wine movies are much harder to name. In fact, most of the movies about wine are rather bad.

I'm not a *Sideways* fan. I think that movie, made over a decade ago, was accorded way too much credit for the explosion of interest in Pinot Noir. It was more like an obnoxious buddy movie to me than a paean to wine. Then there are the movies based on true-to-life wine events, most of which seem more like small- rather than big-screen-worthy events. I'm thinking of movies like *Bottle Shock*, based on the famous Judgment of Paris tasting that pitted French wine against American. Does anyone besides a hardcore oenophile care how that competition played out? (It wasn't even that big a deal when it happened back in 1976; only the winemakers of the time seemed to care.)

The same is true of television shows about wine, most of which function as wine travelogues. I guess that makes sense, since the most interesting fact about wine for most people is where it comes from. Why else would so many people with only a casual interest in wine spend so much time traveling to tasting rooms in cars, in limos, or on bikes? (The latter mode of transportation seems like a particularly dangerous idea to me; bicycles and alcohol are no better combined than cars and alcohol.)

The few wine shows that showed people tasting wine never lasted particularly long, since they were, well, pretty boring. Who wants to watch someone talk about wine and then swirl it around in their mouth? It's like watching someone talk about sex. Wine, like sex, is something best experienced for yourself.

And wine itself is not particularly visual—at least not for long. I can't remember the last time someone talked about a favorite wine in terms of its looks alone. ("It's just the right shade of red.") It's the same way with wine consumption: it isn't something most people want to watch, especially when tasting and spitting is involved.

Wine isn't made to be watched—nor are its drinkers. At least not for very long. I think a two-minute video is ideal. That's just long enough to learn a little bit about wine. And if you're really interested, you can add to your knowledge by reading a book!

Worst Wine Word

JUST AS CERTAIN PEOPLE leave stronger impressions than others, certain observations can linger long after they have been made. Take, for example, what a prominent New York wine merchant said to me many years ago but that I still can't get out of my head. I had asked Joe Salamone, the head wine buyer of Crush Wine & Spirits in Manhattan, to name the one word that buyers used most often to describe the wines that they wanted. He didn't hesitate. "Smooth," he replied. It was the most common and at the same time most useless word.

Smooth could be anything to anyone, observed Mr. Salamone. Smooth had many interpretations—and many incarnations. Does a smooth wine have soft tannins? Or lots of fruit? Red or white or even sparkling? (Can a sparkling wine ever be considered smooth?)

Outside the world of wine, the definition of *smooth* seems clear enough. *Smooth* means "having a regular surface, free of lumps," or, in the case of wine, a flavor that is "free of harshness or bitterness" and that is also "mellow and mild." I find those last two words even more opaque (and actually a bit disagreeable, too, truth be told) when used to characterize wine. A mellow wine suggests it may be so laid back as to be completely devoid of personality or flavor—not unlike a mellow guy. Ditto someone who is mild.

A wine—like a person—requires a bit of friction to be interesting. While in a person that may take the form of strong opinions and firmly held beliefs, with a wine it's structure and acidity. The latter is something that Mr. Salamone says his customers particularly fear, even though every wine needs some amount of acidity to be fully alive. Perhaps wine drinkers should ask for a wine that is "fully alive." It may or may not result in a wine that is smooth, but I guarantee it will be a wine that is interesting.

Why White
Is Better than Red

WHEN THE WORLD OF WINE WRITING was dominated by Englishmen many, many years ago, a waggish English wine writer named Harry Waugh made a proclamation that some still believe to be true. It had to do with the inferiority of white wine. Or as Harry himself said, "The first duty of a wine is to be red." (There was actually a follow-up to that sentence: ". . . the second is to be a Burgundy.")

I know quite a few people who regard this as gospel. Many years ago my older sister declared that she would no longer drink white wine, as it was "unsophisticated," and from that moment forward was committed to red. She drank red wine through the year, during the winter and during the hottest summer—until she moved to Dallas, which happens to be the hottest place in the United States in the summer. She began drinking white wine again and never looked back.

I've never stopped drinking one color or another, but I have lately rediscovered the particular appeal of a refreshing glass of white. In fact, I may be an even bigger fan of white than red wine these days—for a number of reasons.

The first reason is its versatility. Because white wine has very little tannin compared to red wine, it's easier to pair with food. It's particularly good with cheese. In fact, that's one of the big lies of wine and food pairing; white wine and cheese go together much better and more often than red wine and cheese.

White wine is also more refreshing. And lower in alcohol. And it seems to give people fewer problems the day after. I know a lot of people who "can't tolerate" red wine very well—for reasons they're not even sure why, though many cite the histamines in red wine. As to the alcohol levels, there are some white wines like Riesling and Vinho Verde that are frequently below 10 percent alcohol. That means you can drink a lot more white wine and it won't hurt as much afterwards.

White wine is also cheaper. If you don't believe this, look closely at the wine list next time you're in a restaurant and count the number of white wines under fifty dollars and the number of reds under that number. Red wine is almost always more expensive. One reason is that it's more expensive to make—it takes longer to age, and it usually involves the use of oak. And oak is expensive—new French oak barrels can cost as much as a thousand dollars apiece.

There are still reasons to drink red wine, of course. I can't think of many white wines that could do justice to steak on a grill (though an oaky Chardonnay can come close), and there are flavors of a good Grenache or Pinot Noir that just can't be duplicated by a Sauvigon Blanc or a Riesling. But overall—and apologies to Mr. Waugh—I think there are actually a lot more reasons to drink white than red.

The Good and the Great

AMERICANS ARE BIG BELIEVERS in greatness. No American aspires to "pretty good." Greatness is part of our cultural fabric and it's a staple of seemingly every educational program or political talk. Some politicians even write books with the word *great* in large letters in the title, believing that its presence alone is enough to prove that the book itself is more than good.

American oenophiles are equally impassioned about greatness. They like to drink great wine, they like to talk about great wine, and most of all they like to talk about drinking great wine. That's one of the differences between a great wine and a good wine; a great wine needs, above all, to be discussed.

But what exactly constitutes a great wine? And how far is a great wine from a wine that is just good? The two share some of the same qualities. They're both well made and generally pleasurable to drink. But a great wine must possess certain additional and perhaps even ineffable qualities.

A good wine, for example, can be good right out of the gate, while a great wine is obliged to evolve in an even more interesting fashion for many years. A great wine improves with time, gaining complexity and nuance and depth. Of course, unless you've tasted a lot of great wines, this can be hard to detect. Great wine requires a great deal of experience on the part of the drinker. A good wine doesn't require much more of the drinker than a bottle, a corkscrew, and a glass.

A great wine also requires patience. Great wines require leisurely stretches of time and the right storage conditions—ideally a cool (55-degree) cellar that's dark with a moderate amount of humidity. A good wine is much hardier: it doesn't need quite as much cosseting or fancy conditions. It's more like a mum than an orchid or a rose.

A great wine is usually rare and produced in very small quantities. It's almost always hard to find—and/or priced very high, although there are some exceptions (you have to know a lot about great wine to find them). For example, everyone knows that the first growths of Bordeaux are great; the French even created a list to ensure that it was clear: they ranked the estates from first to fifth growth, in (more or less) descending order according to quality and, more importantly, price.

Alas, this is the only system that makes degrees of greatness abundantly clear: there is no other rating system as straightforward as Bordeaux. (No wonder everyone wants to buy them. It's clear who's worth the most: collectors covet first-growth Bordeaux and pay four- or five-figure prices for a case of wine.)

And yet there are plenty of great wines made in less-heralded places, like the Loire Valley of France. There are some truly great wines made in the Loire, notably the Vouvrays from Domaine Huet or Jacky Blot, but collectors don't chase after Loire Valley Chenin Blanc the way they do grand cru Burgundy. There just isn't enough prestige in the pursuit, I suppose.

There is an ineffable quality to greatness, an evanescence that's hard to capture in adjectives alone. It's a wine that seems one way one time and another way another time: greatness isn't necessarily dependable.

A good wine, on the other hand, is easy to comprehend. It doesn't require extensive experience or, for that matter, much thought. A good wine has texture and flavor and is balanced, but the overall impression is more sensual than intellectual. A great wine is more challenging, especially when it comes to capturing it in words. The challenge is similar to explaining why a certain work of art is great—or just good.

I don't drink a lot of great wine, and I own even less. But I have some good friends (and some great friends) who have very good cellars and generous spirits, so I've tasted great wine often enough over the years to recognize when there's one in my glass. That's another happy fact about great wines: the people who own them like to share them with friends. Perhaps it's the same principle as all those politicians and their books: they like to be associated with the word *great*.

Bottle of the Sexes

WHENEVER A COMPANY DECIDES to create a softer, simpler version of a product it's inevitably made with women in mind. Unfortunately, this often includes wine.

Take, for example, Little Black Dress (yes, that's a real wine brand). Clearly there are winemakers—or more likely wine marketers—who think that a woman can best appreciate a wine if it's described in sartorial terms. This particular brand is a veritable closet full of such attire, including a Black Dress Divalicious blend, which contains Pinot Grigio, of course, since it's the grape that women love.

And it gets even worse. There is a brand that hints at a less than healthy relationship between a woman and her bottle (i.e., Mommy's Time Out), and a wine that suggests something that's less than attractive about the woman herself (Bitch wine, anyone?).

And yet there are no equivalent wines for men. There is no Beefcake Syrah or Couch Potato Chenin Blanc or a Channel Changer Chardonnay (sold in a bottle the shape of a remote control, naturally). Is that because all wine is essentially male? Or are men unintimidated by names the way women are? Are they assumed to be knowledgeable just because they are male, the same way that French people are assumed to be stylish because they are French? Are they so secure in their taste that they don't need to be coaxed into buying a bottle by a label adorned with well-tailored pants?

Women actually buy more wine than men—at least in terms of numbers of bottles if not actual bottle worth. A male retailer once explained the power positioning like this: "Men buy Montrachet; women buy Sancerre."

But women also buy much more frequently—and the women I know are far more open to experimentation than the men, who tend to

settle on a certain range of wines if not a particular brand. And women don't care about scores or money the way that men do—they may like a wine, but they don't engage in heated debates or competitions over whose wine is the best. In fact, the only wine arguments I've ever had were with men. Women are much more likely to concede. "Oh, you found that the aromas reminded you of strawberries, not spice? You must be right."

Maybe women should argue more—take positions about what producers are best, brag about their collections, and talk more about scores. Maybe they wouldn't have dopey wines named after dresses made just for them. But then of course they'd be just like men.

The Last Big Thing

SOME WRITERS MANAGE JUST ONE REALLY GOOD BOOK, some actors shine in a single role, and some grapes are sought-after for just a short period of time. I'm thinking of Viognier, of course.

An aromatic white grape native to the Rhône Valley of France and grown in various other parts of the world, Viognier is a grape that many wine professionals—at least briefly—thought would be the Next Big Thing. It was even considered a possible successor to Chardonnay. Alas, like a second book by Harper Lee (*To Kill a Mockingbird*) or a memoir by J. D. Salinger, that never materialized.

The Viognier boom or perhaps more accurately "boomlet" took place in the late 1990s and early 2000s. That's a lifetime ago in terms of world events, but it's a short period of time in winegrowing terms. During the time that Viognier was hot, it was planted in vineyards all over California without special regard to whether or not they were suitable to the grape. It was planted in Napa and Sonoma and the Central Coast, too. It was even planted in Lodi, a hot inland region that's probably best known for Zinfandel—or as the headquarters for Mondavi's Woodbridge wines.

Viognier presents a conundrum of sorts from beginning to end. There is the conundrum of its aromas: powerful scents of apricot and honeysuckle so heady that Viognier is practically the patchouli of grapes. That means for wine drinkers who don't like a wine with a lot of perfume, Viognier can be off-putting in the same way as another scent-heavy grape like Gewürztraminer.

Then there is the matter of how it tastes. Viognier can be quite rich and full-bodied and, under the wrong circumstances and in the wrong hands, it can turn blowsy (think Anna Nicole Smith) and tiresome to drink. That's generally what happens when Viognier is picked too late: the acidity drops and the wine becomes alcoholic and oily. On the other hand, if it's picked too early Viognier won't ripen and so the wine will be a bit lean and shrill—without its usual lush aromas and warmth.

But when the circumstances are ideal and all elements are in balance, Viognier can be a stunning wine—opulent but dry, with beguiling (but not oppressive) aromas that simply billow out of the glass. The wines of Condrieu in the northern Rhône Valley are probably the best examples of Viognier at its peak. But few people are likely to taste Condrieu wines, as the annual production is small (about thirty thousand cases for the entire region) and the wines are expensive (and not well distributed).

Will Viognier ever be as popular as it almost was more than a decade ago? It seems as unlikely as Harper Lee writing a second book. On the other hand, if an author who was not Margaret Mitchell could write a sequel to *Gone With the Wind*, then maybe another grape that's a lot like Viognier (Gewürztraminer? Muscat?) could be the next almost-big thing.

To Your Health

WINE IS GOOD. WINE IS BAD. Wine makes you live longer. Wine cuts your life in half. The health claims—and disclaimers—about wine are confusing and contradictory.

Although wine and health have been intertwined for centuries (people once drank wine because water was dangerous), the first modern instance was the French Paradox, that wonderful if implausible-sounding promise of the 1990s that you could drink red wine *and* eat a diet high in fat—*comme la française*! Wine wasn't just about pairing with food, it was about looking after your heart.

More studies were launched and more cheery health news was issued. A diet high in resveratrol (a compound found in red wine) was reportedly beneficial as well. Wine was found to be good for memory and it perhaps might even help prevent breast cancer. As long as it wasn't too much wine. Then the wine would only make matters worse.

Wine was found to be good for helping to settle the stomach— although it could wreak havoc on your liver if consumed in overlarge amounts. For every purported benefit associated with wine there was a downside looming, perhaps even larger. And, of course, all the benefits could be gained only if the intake of wine was moderate, whatever that meant. No one could agree on the meaning of the word or the amount of wine that could be "safely" consumed. Would that be the next warning label on a bottle, in addition to the cautionary word issued for pregnant women?

In fact, there may be even more information disseminated and opinions expressed worldwide on the meaning of *moderation* in regard to wine than anything related to health. A glass a day for women, two glasses for men are moderate amounts, some researchers have posited, although Europeans would allow more—and certain Puritanical-minded types in this country would probably call for far less. Some even suggested a glass every other day was more than enough—perhaps even borderline "problem drinking." Even my family doctor, Dr. Martin Feuer, said he couldn't safely "prescribe" an amount. As he helpfully pointed out, "Alcohol is a poison." Did I mention he's a nondrinker?

For anyone who is drinking wine purely for its health-giving properties and not the pleasant feeling that it imparts or to better enhance a good meal, I suggest stopping immediately and maybe drink a glass of grape juice instead. And for those who consider first the dangers of wine every time they raise a glass, I suggest they stop as well. Wine is about pleasure, not fear. And for the rest of us, I suggest we stop too—pretending, that is, that we care about diabetes-heart disease-dementia-cancer and admit that what we seek from wine is pure pleasure. I will definitely drink to that.

Fast and Fickle Friends

WHY DO OTHERWISE SENSIBLE PEOPLE seek professional help in drinking a specific wine with a specific dish? Is it insecurity or is it part of a larger quest for perfection? (If a Sauvignon Blanc is good, could a Chardonnay be even better with the fish?) An uncertain diner will seek the sommelier's advice on just the "right" wine in a sea of choices.

And what sort of advice do the experts give? As far as I can tell, it's pretty much all over the place. Some wine professionals might talk in terms of pairing the wine with the main dish (chicken, meat, fish), while others talk in terms of matching the type of sauce (spicy or creamy). Yet others may reference the texture or weight (rich, light, or dense) of the wine or the dish. Yet more might talk in terms of matching all three—a dizzying thought as well as a near impossibility. Of course, you don't need to rely on an actual, live wine professional. There are charts and color wheels and even quizzes intended to help ordinary people pair their wine and food responsibly. And there are a great many books about pairing—one of which actually contains my least favorite piece of advice on the subject: Drink what you like.

The so-called pairing experts like to use words like *fat* and *acidity* (the former in food, the latter in wine). Some say that a wine with a lot of acidity should never be paired with fatty, creamy food, while some counsel exactly the opposite. Then there is the culturally tried and true: You can pair any wine with any food if they were both made in the same part of the world.

So what's the answer? Disappointingly, perhaps, I don't have one. I think that the bond between food and wine is pretty elastic and there aren't many matches that are downright terrible. And you will probably recognize them when they occur. Try drinking a Chianti with oysters and you'll know what I mean. So don't worry: It's not likely to happen, and if it does there's always another wine and another meal.

A Life in Wine

I WAS A TWENTY-YEAR-OLD STUDENT from Ohio when I traveled to Ireland for the very first time. I was hoping to study Irish history and politics. Instead, I fell in love with wine.

The wine wasn't Irish, but my tutor, Peter Dunne, a wine merchant in Dublin, whom I came to call "my Irish father," certainly was. I lived with Peter and his family in their house in Dublin, as one of a long line of American college students who ate the excellent if potato-centric dinners cooked by his wife, Anne, and drank the wines that Peter brought home each night. Peter talked about wine in a way that I'd never heard anyone talk about wine before; there was history and politics and literature—metaphor and simile in every bottle he opened. (My parents drank wine, but the conversation never centered on the contents of the bottle—and considering what they drank, this was just as well.)

From time to time I followed Peter down to the wine shop, Mitchell and Son, in the heart of the city across from the Irish Houses of Parliament. It all seemed so glamorous and so civilized that I decided I wanted to be in "the wine business" too—even if I didn't really know what that meant.

A week after college graduation, I moved to New York to begin my "wine business" career. Things got a bit complicated from there—and crowded with a variety of wine-related jobs. Over a period of ten years or so, I had just about every job in the wine business: retail store clerk, wholesale sales rep, restaurant manager, and even public relations and marketing professional.

Some jobs lasted longer than others, but none seemed like exactly the right fit. (I was a particularly bad salesperson; I was always ready to take "no" for an answer.) It wasn't until I became a wine journalist that my life in the wine business looked like it might actually work out.

As I was learning the wine business during those years, the wine business was changing a great deal. The wine critic Robert M. Parker, Jr., was on the brink of fame when I got my first wine job (retail store clerk) and he soon became the arbiter of seemingly every wine that was produced in the world.

The wines of Bordeaux were the only ones that wine drinkers seemed to care much about in those faraway days (but Mr. Parker was a big fan) save perhaps for some high-profile Burgundies and big Champagne houses. Now people openly wonder if Bordeaux is passé. Burgundy has transitioned from a wine to be enjoyed at the table to a wine that only billionaires can afford to buy, let alone drink. The wines of the Rhône were obscure, and no one much cared about Châteauneuf-du-Pape until Mr. Parker did, and now those wines are some of the most sought-after in the world.

California Cabernets were just beginning to come into their own in the late 1980s and early 1990s, and now they've been supplanted by California Chardonnay, Pinot Noir, and varietal oddities like Trousseau. Syrah has come and gone several times in California too. I don't know where it is now or if it will ever (really) return. Wines from other California regions besides Napa started showing up on wine shelves and restaurants; Paso Robles, Santa Barbara, Anderson Valley, and the Sonoma coast all become "hot" for a period of time—and many have remained so to this day.

Oregon and Washington became well respected and well established, and even the wines of New York have gotten some respect lately (especially Riesling). And Europe? Is there a country whose wines aren't imported or an importer who isn't looking to represent the very last unimported great talent from . . . Moravia? Yes, there is even a wine importing company specializing in Moravian wines too.

And every last region of Italy and France has been plundered by wine importers and, later, especially hipster somms. There isn't a single multisyllabic Italian grape that hasn't found a home on a restaurant wine list in Brooklyn. The wines of Spain cycle in and out of desirability, as do the wines of Australia and New Zealand. Argentina continues to coast on the coattails of Malbec. Will Americans ever get tired of drinking Malbec? And can Malbec help prevent Argentina's (next) economic crisis?

Wine prices go up and come down, fake wines are possibly everywhere, and great deals abound. (You can still get some really good wine for less than fifteen dollars and occasionally some good wines for ten.) So much has changed, is changing, and will change once again in "the wine business," and I hope to bear witness to it all.

Index

Acknowledgments

There are many people who have helped make this book possible and who have been sources of inspiration, in wine and in life. Thanks first and foremost to my brilliant editors at *The Wall Street Journal* and the guiding forces behind that great newspaper. Thanks to my friends who have happily shared many delicious—and not so delicious—bottles over the years and always had something interesting and quotable to say about them. Thanks to the brilliant team behind this book—editor Christopher Steighner, designer Alison Lew, illustrator Robb Burnham, and my agent Alice Martell. Thank you to Alan Richman, the A. J. Liebling of today (with many more James Beard Awards). And finally, thank you to all the remarkably talented and hardworking men and women in the wine business—the winemakers, winery owners, retailers, importers, and sommeliers who have given me so much to write about for so long.

Cheers!

About the Author

LETTIE TEAGUE is a staff writer and wine columnist at *The Wall Street Journal*. She was formerly the wine columnist of *Food & Wine* for ten years and its wine editor for twelve years. She is the author of *Educating Peter* and the coauthor of *Fear of Wine*. She has won three James Beard Awards, including the M. F. K. Fisher Distinguished Writing Award.